My Mother and Me

My Mother and Me

Making It in New York

After Making It

Out of Berlin and Beirut

Peter Edward Schrag, M.D.

Published 2018
Printed in the United States of America
Print ISBN: 978-0-9998564-0-6
E-ISBN: 978-0-9998564-1-3
Library of Congress Control Number: 2018901197

Cover and interior design by Tabitha Lahr

Dedication

This book is dedicated to my children and grandchildren. My children were in their late twenties or early thirties when Karl and Ilse Schrag died, so they knew their grandparents and remember them well. However, some earlier events and reminiscences of earlier times in their lives may be worth relating.

Every spring my children and their families get together and read from the Haggadah, which tells the story of the exodus from Egypt. The flight of Jews from Europe and the exodus of German Jews from Germany in the years 1933-1941 was a twentieth-century Exodus. Jews left for France, North Africa, Turkey, China, Mexico, Cuba, Brazil, Argentina, Uruguay, South Africa, Canada, and the United States. The United States was the promised land in the late 1930s. This memoir was written to record some of the details of my mother's story but not because her story is very different or particularly unusual or more interesting than the story of any number of others. It was written only because it is our own particular story, which I happen to know in some detail.

"If you say or do A and B, you may have to accept, say, or do C."

—Maxim of Ilse Szamatiolski/Preiss/Price/Schrag

"Look," said the proud mother as she was watching a military parade, "the whole army is marching out of step except for my son."

—A favorite joke of Ilse's

"Real truth lies, if anywhere, not in facts but in nuances."

—John Le Carré (pen name of the former spy and author John Cornwall)

"We should beware of the error of judging eras and places according to the prevailing standards of the here and now."

—Primo Levi

"What is familiar is not known simply because it is familiar."

—Hegel

CHAPTER I:

Revisiting Difficult Decisions·

My mother, Ilse Szamatolski, has been dead for twenty
years. She lived from December 2nd, 1910 until November 26th, 1997. Her life spanned the twentieth century almost
in its entirety. I am somewhat reluctant to write about her life
for the same reason I am reluctant to read the four-volume
biography of Lyndon Baines Johnson by Robert Caro. I do
not think that at this time in my life I need to take up so
much of my time thinking about LBJ. My reservations about
LBJ are based on my belief that Johnson erred in his judgment about the most important problem of his era, the war
in Viet Nam—the war that affected my generation, cost the
life of my friend and colleague Dr. Howard Gerstel, and cost
the lives of thousands of others. (The Viet Nam Veterans'
Memorial to Americans who died in Viet Nam is a black wall
150 yards long and contains over 58,000 names. If a similar
monument were built with the same density of names for the
Vietnamese who died in the Viet Nam War, it would be more
than nine miles long. See *Nothing Ever Dies: Viet Nam and the
Memory of War* by Viet Thanh Nguyen, Harvard University

Press, 2016, page 66.) I avoided Viet Nam by serving in the U.S. Public Health Service in lieu of military service, with the rank of Lt. Commander, the equivalent of being a Major in the U.S. Army. I may eventually pick up Caro's biography, as it is said to be superb. But in this home, at least for now, it remains unread.

The relevance of all this to my thoughts about my mother's life is that she, too, was forced to deal with some problems as major in her era as the Viet Nam war was during the time of LBJ's presidency. She spent the years 1910-1933 in Germany, mainly in Berlin, and did not get caught in the Europe of World War II. How she managed her life and the resulting consequences obviously influenced me and how I managed my own life. Did I, or do I, admire her? Unquestionably I do admire her, and I also loved her. For many years she was the most important person in my life.

I was born in 1938, and from the earliest times that I can remember until 1945, when she remarried, she was the only parent I had. When I think of those years I remember I often felt that it was she and I against the rest of the outside world. What was she like, how did we manage together, and how did I escape from her controlling influence (assuming I eventually did so)? Perhaps this is worth writing about, despite my reluctance to admit that her personality and her influence on my life still preoccupy me at times even at this late stage of my life.

I am without question the only person in the world who sees an analogy between the life and personality of Ilse Szamatolski/Price/Schrag and that of Lyndon Baines Johnson. What on earth am I thinking of or referring to? Am I joking? Perhaps I am joking somewhat, but not entirely. The analogous or similar traits that they had in common which come to mind, and which are obvious to me—even if this strange sounding analogy between my mother and LBJ has never occurred to anyone else—are as follows. Both were powerful personalities who did a great deal of good. Both were lively, capable, highly intelligent, worldly, keen observers of others, skilled and highly aggressive manipulators of other people, and highly adept at zeroing in on the foibles or weaknesses of others and using this knowledge to their advantage when it suited their purposes. Both were disingenuous when they needed to be, and both were loyal to their supporters and values. Both had to deal with much condescension—LBJ from the Kennedy family, my mother from her own family. Both did a great deal of harm to the very people they loved, due to a blind spot or a critical decision that they had made carefully and deliberately but which was faulty or needed revision in the long run. These decisions most likely were justifiable at the time they were made, but both my mother and LBJ were unable to revisit some critical, previously made decisions—thereby, in Ilse's case, making life harder than it should have been for loved ones, specifically for me. Both LBJ and my mother came to realize that they were "wrong"— about the war in his case, and in my mother's case, in regard to the handling of her divorce and the subsequent ostracism and banishment of her first husband, my biological father, from my life.

CHAPTER 2:

Roots in Berlin and Germany

I am looking at a document stamped by the "polizeipraes-ident-Berlin," i.e. the police chief's office in Berlin, dated October 19, 1933. It is a certificate of citizenship, a *"Hei-matschein" (fur den aufenhalt im Ausland)*, which is an exit visa for a trip outside of Germany to another country. At the top is an eagle, and above the eagle is written *"Deutsches Reich, Preussen."* The document reads that Fraulein Ilse Szamatolski, born on "Dezember" 2, 1910 in Charlottenburg, *"besitzt die Staatsangehorigkeit in Preussen und ist somit Deutsche"* ("Miss Ilse Szamatolski, born December 2, 1910, possesses the status of belonging to the state of Prussia and is thereby German"). The document is valid until October 19, 1934 (*Diese Bescheini-gung gilt bis zum 19. Oktober, 1934*). There is an official stamp that cost two reichmarks. My mother signed the document at the bottom, where it says, *"Der Inhaber hat den heimatsch-ein, ehe er ihn einer auslandishen behoerde vorlegt, eigenhaendig zu unterschrreiben"* (The person indicated is required to sign the document in his own handwriting before placing it into the hands of a foreign official). My mother was twenty-two years old and she needed this document to leave for Beirut, Lebanon to visit Dr. Hans Preiss, a twenty-nine-year-old gynecologist whom she would marry in December 1933, almost exactly one month after her mid-November arrival in Beirut. Ilse had visited Hans Preiss's parents in Kattowitz for a week shortly before she left for Beirut. She traveled from Berlin to Beirut with her mother. She said goodbye to her father, a sixty-five-year-old man. At the time she said good-bye to him, she did not know or imagine she would never see again; he died suddenly from a heart attack in 1935.

Hitler had come to power in Germany in January of 1933 and Nazis were parading in the streets, singing songs such as *"Wenn das Juden blut vom messer spritzt"* ("When Jewish blood spurts forth from the knife"). No doubt Ilse was going to Beirut to marry Hans Preiss (M.D. 1928, University of Berlin, born in 1904), whom she had met in Berlin. It was also an opportune time for a Jewish girl to leave Germany. I never saw the exit visa I described above until after my mother had died, when I went through old papers. What impresses me now is that she was only twenty-two years old when she decided to leave her home. The document also serves as a reminder that she was unquestionably not only "German," but a Prussian born in the Charlottenburg district of Berlin (named after Sophia Charlotte of Hanover [1668-1705], wife of King Fredrick I of Prussia). The Prussians are not only German but are even a bit more exacting and particular and insistent on formalities, and may also be "tougher," "stricter," or more demanding than other Germans. No doubt the autumn of 1933 was an auspicious time to leave Berlin; my mother's timing was good. (I use the word "auspicious" quite deliberately. The word means favorable or conducive to suc-cess, and comes from the French or Latin *auspex*, an observer of birds, a word derived and compounded from *avis* [bird] and *specere* [to look]; it originally referred to divination or prophesy derived from observing birds in flight. The decision to go to Beirut from Berlin in 1933 was "flight" and was thought at the time to be "conducive to success," as the auguries for Jewish life in Berlin were not favorable in 1933).

My maternal grandparents lived on the Kaiserdamm Strasse in Berlin and were upper middle class. Albert Szamatolski was born in 1868 and was fifty in December 1918. His fiftieth birthday party was canceled as Berlin was in the midst of a revolution, the Kaiser was being ousted, and the streets were not safe. Albert worked for Reiffenberg and Soehne (Reiffenberg and sons), a trimmings business. Working in the textile industry and related businesses was a common occupation for Jews in those days in Berlin. In 1933 Hitler came to power, and the Jewish Reiffenbergs tried to preserve their business by "aryanizing" it, i.e. firing their Jewish employees. Albert Szamatolski lost his job in 1934 or 1935. His son, my mother's only brother, born in 1906, was dismissed from his job in the civil service as a lawyer/prosecutor in 1933, as Jews could no longer work in the civil service. He went to work for his father-in-law, a well-to-do paper manufacturer.

I did not hear much about Berlin from my mother, nor much about my grandfather, but I knew my grandfather had a car before the first world war. He did not drive, as he had a chauffeur. Dr. Hans Preiss said to me in 1974 that he thought Albert, my maternal grandfather, was a financial genius, made much money in the stock market, and was well off. Of the three children, my mother—the youngest—never was interested in investing money, although both her brother and her sister spent time every business day investing in or selling shares. They did this all their lives, collaborating together over the telephone before they bought or sold shares. They had been taught by their father. My mother was critical of her siblings for spending so much of their life on the phone discussing stocks. She was excluded from their intimacy, which possibly contributed to her being annoyed with their preoccupation.

For both Susie and Henry, the idea of including Ilse in their discussions about the stock market would have been ridiculous. They did not think Ilse was interested or capable in this regard and, although they were correct, this attitude of theirs gradually evolved into chronic condescension towards their little sister. (Hans was four years older than my mother, and Susie was two years older than Hans.) This condescension was hidden by loyalty, love, and kindness, but I noticed it and thought they underrated my mother's intelligence. My mother, in turn, condescended towards them—not in underrating their intelligence, which she always respected, but in bemoaning their limited cultural interests and knowledge. In this my mother was correct, and her sister Susie would admit she preferred the company of *geschaeft's leute*, business or commercial people. My mother's sister and brother knew that Ilse, as the youngest, was doted on by her father. My mother told me her father had often said to her that she need not worry about any problems in life: he would take care of her, and she need only stay close to him. Then my mother would laugh and say, "It turned out to be all quite different from what he had predicted."

I think my mother had a good life as a child. The family had a full-time cook; my grandmother only cooked on Sundays, the cook's day off. When they were little there was a nanny, a *kindermaedschen* (in German, literally "a girl for the children"). My mother told me that she and her siblings were fond of "Rosa." My mother had a close friend her own age who lived in the same building, a girl called Hanni (from Johannah). Hanni and my mother stayed friends all their lives. As a boy in the early 1940s, I remember my mother sending packages of food to Hanni in London. Hanni once said to me that the wrapping used by Americans always astounded the

English, but that when it came to wrapping tea the Americans really went too far. They did not realize tea bags were meant to be put into the water and were not just "wrapping."

I spoke with Hanni on the phone in 1997, after my mother died. Hanni talked to me at length about my maternal grandfather, whom she knew well; he read stories to her and my mother when they were little girls. Hanni said he was a cultured man and an intellectual who was interested in politics, literature, and history. Then she added, "Quite unlike your grandmother." My mother said life had been hard during the first world war, which she remembered as she turned eight years old two weeks after it ended in November of 1918. My mother recalls following horses and collecting the dung to use as fertilizer, which was hard to come by in wartime. As far as my mother was concerned, the most important consequence of the arrival of automobiles in Berlin at the beginning of the century was that there was less horse manure, which had dotted the streets of Berlin and created a pervasive stench.

My mother and her brother Hans were seventeen and twenty-one, respectively, when they travelled for a few days on the Neckar River by "Klepper" boat. The "Klepper boats" were collapsible kayaks, first designed in 1905 by an architecture student named Alfred Heurich but later manufactured by Johannes Klepper in a factory in Rosenheim, Germany. They are still sold ubiquitously. The Neckar is a 221-mile-long river and tributary of the Rhine that runs through Baden north past Heidelberg to Mannheim, where it joins the Rhine. My mother told me several times that she had a skirt to wear but forgot to take a slip, so when they went to a town her brother was embarrassed by the relatively transparent skirt she wore.

At Ilse's funeral service, at the end of November 1997, her brother—my uncle Henry Samton, who was then ninety years old—said to me just as we were going into the service, "Did I ever tell you about our trip on the Neckar?"

I said, "The story about the transparent skirt?"

"No, not that story," he replied, "the story about the concierge at the inn. We would camp out for several nights and then would check into a hotel for a night where there was a shower or a bath. As we checked in at a local inn the concierge asked, 'One room or two?' 'Two,' I said. 'She is my sister.' 'Oh, I will put you in one room, we are not so prudish here,' replied the concierge. 'But she really is my sister,' said her brother. The concierge waved him away saying, 'You don't have to make up stories for me. Have a good time.'" I had never heard that story before; we laughed, and then proceeded into the memorial service.

CHAPTER 3:

Leftist Sentiments

One of my mother's closest friends was a woman called Edith Lowenstein. Ilse and Edith were childhood friends in Berlin and went skiing together in the late 1920s. After emigrating to the United States, Edith became a lawyer and worked as an immigration lawyer for the U.S. Department of Justice. After some years she went into private practice, defending criminals whom the government wanted to deport. My earliest recollection of Edith is from 1943 or 1944, when I was five or six years old. Edith came with my mother to visit me in Island Park one weekend afternoon and brought me a gift, a helmet and a toy machine gun with a tripod on which to position it. There was some discussion as to whether this was an appropriate gift for a five- or six-year-old but Edith said clearly I liked it and, therefore, I should have it. Years later, and for all the time I lived at 127 East 95th Street (from 1947 to 1955, when I left for college), Edith was a frequent guest for supper. Karl always insisted Edith not be invited with anyone else; she did not like to listen to others, lived alone, and regaled us with stories about criminals whom she had helped and kept from being deported, and who would then invite her to their homes. Some sounded rather unsavory, and she would laugh as she described how she had dined with some very grateful gangster. Karl never found this very interesting, but Ilse and I liked Edith and her stories, and I was always favorably disposed towards family friends who had once given me an interesting gift.

Edith had no family, but had had a brother whom she loved and who fought against Franco in 1936-1937; he died in Spain in the civil war. Ilse had known him and had thought highly of him. My inclination to respect "socialists" probably began with the quiet and respectful way my mother spoke about Edith's brother. I do not think my politics were greatly affected, but I did assimilate a respect for political values and learned that sometimes it was even necessary to die for them.

In 1958, Karl and Ilse wanted to go to Spain, which was still ruled by Franco. I said I would not go if we were going to spend money in Spain and help Franco's economy. That was nonsense, of course, as what we would spend (about $5000) was of no consequence to the Spanish economy. The United States had airplane bases in Spain and paid Franco a great deal of money, which *did* have significant economic importance for Spain. But my mother consulted her brother, who did business in Spain with Jimmy Baehr (formerly Baehrwald), a cousin on the Szamatolski side. My uncle explained we would not have to spend any money in Spain. It worked as follows: in those days it was illegal to take money out of Spain to buy dollars, or to take dollars out of Spain. So the plan was for us to visit Jimmy Baehr in his office in Barcelona; he would give us as many pesetas as we wanted, and on our return to New York we would deposit the equivalent of what we had taken from him, exchanged into dollars, into an account for Jimmy's benefit to use when he came to the U.S.A. When I first heard of this I said, "That cannot be legal." But my uncle asked who in the Spanish government would or could find out about any of this. The answer was "no one," so we would help Jimmy get money out of Spain and would add no dollars to the Spanish economy. Reassured that I would not be helping the Spanish economy obtain more United States dollars, I agreed to go to Spain.

CHAPTER 4:

De Mortuiis Nihil Nisi Bene:
Speak Only Well of the Dead

$\mathcal{B}$efore proceeding further with these thoughts and rec-
ollections, I have to ask myself how can I write all this
down. My mother might have been horrified to know that
anyone might read such personal information, or my very
personal evaluation and reminiscences of her life. I can hear
her say, as she said of the memoirs written by Hans Preiss
(her husband from 1933-1938), "nothing but lies." At this
moment I think there is some justification for my recording
my thoughts; Ilse has been dead for nineteen years, and what
I remember exists only in my memory unless I write it down.
It will not exist at all if I do not write down some of these
thoughts, events, and relationships. Karl has been dead for
over twenty years and cannot be embarrassed or annoyed,
Hans Preiss has been dead for over forty years and cannot be
offended, and the older generation is gone (with the exception
of Susie Schrag, who lives alone with full-time assistance and
was 106 in November, 2016; anyway, she can no longer raise

objections—even Susie cannot be critical of others forever). I now represent the older (or oldest) generation, and I loved my mother, so I doubt this will be "hateful" or disparaging to a significant degree.

I am also putting together thoughts in regard to a person who navigated through treacherous times in a very tumultuous century. My mother moved from Berlin, Germany to Beirut, Lebanon (neither place was idyllic at the time she lived there, or since), and then to New York City. I recall that, in her old age—when New York City had serious problems (such as murders; garbagemen on strike with garbage accumulating in the streets; water shortages that had become acute; fights between Blacks and Jews, whose neighborhoods adjoined one another in Brooklyn and who occasionally attacked one another or accidentally drove cars into one another, causing riots to erupt because some child or infant had been badly injured; or the construction of a large mosque at the corner of 97th Street and Second Avenue, two blocks from her brownstone house, where dozens of taxis driven by Muslim taxi drivers who had stopped off to pray to Mecca were lined up on both sides of the street)—my mother would say, "New York City is getting more like Beirut every day."

The cultural adjustments alone between Berlin, Beirut, and New York may be a story worth telling. For now I am writing this to be read only by myself and Jeanette. Perhaps I will eventually have something that will turn out to be worth showing to my children. I recall—from a course given by Mark De Wolf Howe (Professor of Constitutional Law at Harvard Law School, the last law clerk of Supreme Court Justice Oliver Wendell Holmes), a course for undergraduates I took in 1956, when I was a sophomore at Harvard College, called "The Development of the Law of Defamation and Libel in Anglo-American Law," a course Professor Howe was developing, I believe, for his law school students—that one cannot libel the dead, as libel law is based on proving injury and it is hard to injure someone if the person is already dead. Philosophers doubt whether a tree falling in a forest makes a sound if no one is there to hear it; libel law is analogous in that it requires someone to be alive before accepting that speaking ill of someone amounts to a libel or an injury. My mother would not have agreed with the law of libel; she would have said one can injure someone's reputation and memory even after they are dead, and libel laws should protect the dead as well as the living. She believed in the Latin proverb, *De Mortuis nihil nisi bene* (of the dead say nothing unless it is good, i.e. only speak well of the dead), and quoted it on occasion. I only partially agree with her, in that understanding someone requires looking at positives and negatives.

I neither think nor fear that my mother will return or seek vengeance for what I write here. Moreover, my mother would most probably not have objected to my recording my ideas about her life and her times. My mother might have liked to have some of her ideas preserved for her grandchildren, even if her ideas are only transmitted through me. She did not like stereotypes, believed much information was simply misinformation, and believed that people, and especially women, did not get the credit they deserved for their accomplishments. She also believed that the younger generations really do not and cannot understand the past properly without input from the older generation, and that having the older generation teach the younger was worth doing.

My mother also thought that subjects such as what it means to be Jewish—or German, or German and Jewish, or what it was like to live in Germany in the 1930s—were viewed simplistically by subsequent generations, whether because of propaganda, nationalistic or ethnic stereotypes, poor information, or lack of genuine interest. So perhaps she might not object all that much to my recording and interpreting what I recall from her life.

I also remember that very little was ever said by my grandmother about her husband, my maternal grandfather, who died in 1935. That was partly because my grandmother did not "look back." (It may also have been because she did not have happy memories of her marriage—as I inferred from her telling us often that, although widowed before the age of fifty, she never remarried because "once was enough"). Regrets about "what might have been" were avoided by refugees who had been uprooted and who had made a new start in a new country. I think suppressing or repressing the past was necessary to help them enter into a new life. It was counterproductive and also too painful to linger on the losses of the past or previous existence, which had often been, or even had usually been, a more affluent or more sumptuous lifestyle than what the new surroundings offered. Forgetting the past was necessary, at least for a while, until economic circumstances were ameliorated by assimilation, better jobs, or better times. This was usually true, at least in the early stages or phases after relocating to a new country. Looking back is often dismal while the future looks bright and one is appropriately much preoccupied with it.

CHAPTER 5:

Cultural Affinities and Interests

My children, and Kathy Schrag Wangh's children, tended to think of their grandmother as an elderly Germanic lady. In the case of Kathy's kids, this was in part because their other grandmother, their paternal grandmother, was born and raised in the USA. They were (or so it seemed to me) not aware that Ilse was actually very patriotic and a great believer in the USA. On several occasions, my mother would say that it does not matter who you were or where you come from: "Any new immigrant to the United States is better off than he was in his native country ten years after coming to the United States, irrespective of their previous status or employment. That's just the way it is." So she understood America in a very fundamental way and believed in it. What was deemed "Germanic" by my children was possibly related to being German, but I actually think it was also because my mother was a social snob who could be fussy about forms and formalities. I once got into a great deal of trouble because, when I was in college, I called a day late for Karl's birthday. My explanation, that I had an exam, was not an acceptable excuse. My mother often said, "I grew up in Berlin and lived in New York City; I do not want to vote for a president who comes from a small town where there is not even a subway." She always voted Democratic, but this comment was her objection to having to vote for President Jimmy Carter.

I am quite aware that there is much in my mother's life about which I knew or still know nothing. This became apparent one day as I was walking to her house along Lexington Avenue between 94th and 95th Streets, a block from her home. It was approximately 5:00 p.m., and I was on my way to have coffee with her. That was something I did usually on Tuesdays and Thursdays on my way home from work. This was in 1996, when she was a widow. I had learned it was easier for her and for me if she knew exactly when to expect me and I had trained her to let me go after forty-five minutes or so. She often asked me to repair something in her house. I let her pick anything she wished but limited her to one job per visit. She liked being able to assign work to me to show she was still in charge, even if only symbolically. If the chore or job was more than I could easily handle, I could arrange for someone else to do it or defer it to the weekend when I could come and stay until I finished the job.

I was a bit early for my appointment with her that day. There was a small candy store on Lexington Avenue that also sold soft drinks, magazines, and ice cream. She was sitting inside talking to the elderly Arab store owner. I stepped inside. They were engrossed in conversation. I listened and then realized that they were speaking in Arabic. I waited, and after their conversation had ended we walked out together. I recall saying that I had known my mother all of my fifty-nine years but did not know she spoke Arabic. "There is a lot you do not know," she reminded me—quite unnecessarily, I might add. "I lived in Beirut for five years. I learned to speak French but I also learned to speak Arabic," she said. What was significant, but which I had too much tact or consideration to bring up, was that in the fifty-and-a-half years she was married to Karl never once did she utter a sound in Arabic, or say an Arabic phrase, or indicate anything about her ability to speak Arabic. She hid it, as she did not want it to intrude on Karl or remind him (or herself) of her previous life.

My mother surprised me another time by saying she greatly enjoyed *La Cage aux Folles*, which was a successful play on Broadway about a gay couple who run a nightclub, specialize in putting on exhibitions "in drag" (cross-dressing), and have a son whose girlfriend's parents are ultra-conservative. ("La cage aux folles" means "the house of mad women," but "folles" is also a French slang term for effeminate homosexuals, i.e. "queens.") She said she had gone to see it six times. I could hardly believe it. "Why on earth did you go to see this play six times?" I asked. "I just loved it," was my mother's answer.

My mother did love going to the theater. When I was in high school, she often encouraged me to go with a friend to a Broadway show and buy "standing room" tickets at the last minute. These tickets were cheap; we were in high school, and did not mind standing up throughout the performance while leaning on the railing behind the back row of the orchestra. I saw many good plays at little cost. Some were of considerable political significance, including *Antigone* by the French playwright Jean Anouilh and *The Male Animal*, a play in which an English professor is not allowed to read a statement in an English class as an example of fine prose written eloquently by a non-professional poorly-educated man because it was written by the convicted anarchist Vanzetti professing his innocence. (This play was also made into a movie starring Henry Fonda and Olivia De Havilland.)

My mother also liked taking me and one of my cousins to see the movies in the theater in the basement of the Museum of Modern Art on 53rd Street on Saturday afternoons. Those movie tickets were free for members of the museum. We saw almost every Harold Lloyd movie, every Buster Keaton movie, and almost every Charlie Chaplin movie there in the early 1950s. There were also interesting documentaries, newsreels, and an occasional contemporary feature, such as Gregory Peck in *Twelve O'Clock High*.

Karl seldom came with us to see movies at MOMA, although he liked Chaplin movies. If Karl came along, we would stop off after the movie at Schraft's, a well-known Fifth Avenue restaurant/institution in those days, for a strawberry ice cream sundae, which was a favorite of Karl's. But my mother never took us to Schraft's if Karl was not with us; she preferred that we have something she would provide for us at home, which she thought would be preferable to whatever we might order at Schraft's.

I could usually distinguish what was primarily an interest of my mother's from what was mainly an interest of Karl's. But this was not always the case. Karl and Ilse would go to Times Square on New Year's Eve and said they enjoyed being among the crowd. I recall being concerned about whether they would be safe when they did this, especially when they both were in their late seventies. But they both said it was fun and a good way to start the New Year, and they seemed to manage their way through the crowds.

I gather my grandfather had been an interesting and intelligent man; the fact that nothing much was said about him during my lifetime was a pity. Relatively little was said about my biological father for the first thirty-four years of my life, and that too was a mistake. So I have decided to continue to reflect and record things I remember from my mother's life, because I have learned that suppressing things is not always desirable and involves hidden costs.

CHAPTER 6:

Swimming, Tennis, and Hiking

My maternal grandparents would go to Switzerland, to St. Moritz, for several weeks each summer. My mother was a good swimmer, and at age seventeen won a race for guests at the hotel. She remained an avid swimmer for the rest of her life; she believed it was good for her health to swim, swam regularly even in her eighties when she summered in Maine, and went swimming daily in the cold ocean water in Deer Isle with her friend and neighbor Jane Weiss. Ilse insisted her children and grandchildren put on bathing suits and go swimming whenever they visited Maine, even when they did not really want to.

One summer in St. Moritz she also met the Hugo Schrag family. They stayed at the same hotel where her family vacationed. She met Hugo and Bella Schrag, the parents of Paul, Karl, Otto, and Fred. Otto and Fred (Fritz) were their two older sons. She also met an American cousin, V. Henry Rothschild, the only child and son of Bella Sulzberger Schrag's sister Lily, who visited his cousins on several vacations. Many years later, when Lily had just died, Paul Schrag—Lily's nephew, who was a lawyer specializing in wills and estates, as had been his father and as would be his youngest son, and who was the lawyer handling his aunt Lily's estate—expressed some anger at his cousin V. Henry for demanding both an executor's fee and his share of his mother's estate as a beneficiary. My mother's comment at the time was that V. Henry was always devious, disingenuous, conniving, and untrustworthy. She knew this from his tennis game: according to my mother, he never hit the ball cleanly when he played tennis, even when he was a young man. His tennis strokes were always sliced, or cut, or simply eased limply just over the net. Ilse believed one could learn a great deal about people from the way they played games or did sports, and tennis in particular revealed one's character. If someone was unwilling to lose, that was particularly significant; she disapproved of "sore losers." She was good at tennis, ice skating, and swimming, and she could ski. She tried to get her children to do the same, with some success; I was a good ice skater, a good swimmer, and an avid tennis player, but never went skiing regularly and gave it up early in my life. Ilse and Karl and I often went ice skating together, and she and Karl could dance together on the ice, as he could skate backwards. I too learned to skate backwards, which turned out to be socially useful. When I was in high school, I would skate with a girl and she would skate forwards while I would hold her hands and skate backwards on the ice. Therefore I was popular with some of the girls in my class when we went out as a group and skated together at Wollman Rink in Central Park on Friday evenings.

For many years Ilse played tennis on the courts in Central Park. She played with Karl once or twice every season. She took me to the handball courts when I was eight or nine years old, and I hit a tennis ball against the wall of the handball court. Once I could hit a reasonably consistent and forceful forehand stroke, we moved onto the full court. My first own seasonal tennis permit, which I got in 1950 at age twelve, cost $2.50; some years later it went up to $3.50. (Today a season permit costs $200.00, but seniors pay only $20.00.) Ilse played on the Central Park courts with Karl and with her friend Marguerite Goldschmidt. In 1948 and 1949, when Kathy and Juliet were still in baby carriages, they parked the carriages just outside the fence of the side-end court, and left the babies there in the carriages while they played tennis for an hour. Nowadays this would be unacceptable and would be called "child abuse." But it worked then.

My mother almost never played tennis with me after I was about fourteen years old. She believed boys and men should play with men, as men hit the ball harder. At the hotel on the Costa Brava, when I was twenty, I played with a young woman who was a good tennis player and who beat me. My mother watched us play and said this woman might beat me, but that she did not hit the ball hard enough and it would be better for me to find a male to play with. I actually agreed with her and found another partner. In the summer of 1948 there was a tennis tournament at the "Golf Club" in Castine, Maine, where we had rented a substantial and comfortable house because Kathy was a baby and that seemed advisable. I remember that my mother entered the mixed doubles competition at the golf club, where they also had two tennis courts; I watched her and her partner—not Karl, but someone to whom she had been assigned—advance nicely through two or three rounds. I was suitably impressed and surprised. She was thirty-seven years old and I was ten, and I was proud of her.

Ilse believed that after one finished playing tennis, one needed to put on a sweater or sweatshirt to prevent getting chilled. As a boy I was skeptical that this was really necessary on a hot day, but my mother said it was. She insisted that on hot days one sweated even more, and that therefore the likelihood of a chill was greater and the need for putting a sweater on when one had stopped playing was greater. She insisted that, even in very cold weather, one could or should play with just a polo shirt and reserve wearing the sweater or sweatshirt one had brought along until after one had stopped playing. I think she was right. Now, on very hot summer days, when Jeanette wonders if I should even be playing at all in that eighty or ninety degree heat, I take a sweat shirt with me to wear after I have stopped playing. If I am asked, "Do you really need such a warm sweater on such a hot day?" I simply say, "I do." Explaining that this is what my mother drilled into me is not really necessary, although that is the correct answer.

In the 1950s, tennis, skiing, swimming, knapsacks, wearing shorts, mountain climbing and hiking, and wearing shoes or hiking boots with high binding above the ankle were all somewhat tainted with being vaguely European or Germanic. Wealthy people were more likely to play tennis or ski than the middle class. The middle-class kids played baseball, not tennis. They did not go skiing. All that changed a few years later. Now it seems strange to think that in my childhood tennis was something I did to please my European parents, but it was not something I ever mentioned to my school friends. In high school, a classmate with wealthy grandparents took me to their club on Long Island where we played tennis. Today, hiking and wearing a knapsack (once called a "rucksack," as it was worn on one's *rucken*—"back" in German—and which is now called a "backpack") is as American as hot dogs, apple pie, and Chevrolet, as are skiing, tennis, hiking, and mountain climbing. Quite possibly John F. Kennedy deserves some credit for all this, as he campaigned for fitness in the USA and bemoaned a generation of unfit "couch potatoes." But without question, hiking was once looked upon as something "Germanic." Only the Rockefellers, who had a nearby estate, and European Germanic types, often in lederhosen, hiked in Acadia National Park fifty or sixty years ago.

This reminds me: one day, hiking up a small mountain in Acadia National Park, Ilse and Karl came upon an elderly or middle-aged couple sitting on some rocks. He looked tired and exhausted. My mother recognized him; he was David Rockefeller. She offered him some lemon drops, which she always carried and which she extolled for providing energy and refreshment, and he accepted one and thanked her. Later that day my mother said she and Karl had met David Rockefeller and his wife, and my mother would later embellish this meeting by adding she had "saved his life."

CHAPTER 7:

Chanterelles/Pfifferlinge

One of the Germanic pastimes that did not really exist in the USA in 1945 was to hunt for *pfifferlinge*—this being a characteristically orange mushroom that is found in the mossy areas of the Maine woods in August after a rainy day. They have a very distinctive odor and the underside is corrugated, with the furrows leading out from the stem. Ilse would make a delicious cream of mushroom soup with *pfifferlinge* that we picked, and she also made delicious *pfifferlinge* omelets with parsley. The French name for these mushrooms is "chanterelle." Karl and Ilse found these mushrooms in Maine in 1945; they were certain that they had identified them correctly, and ate a batch that they put into some scrambled eggs. They had not fed any to me, thinking that if they made a mistake I should not suffer; but they did not get sick, and from then on we found chanterelles/*pfifferlinge* every summer.

Karl and I occasionally competed as to who could find the most in a fixed period of time as we scrambled through the woods. In the last two decades there has been so much interest in mushrooms and exploring nature that all of the artists in Deer Isle pick chanterelles now, and they are harder to find. My folks also thought they were knowledgeable in regard to another mushroom, something called a *steinpiltze*, but they were less certain they could distinguish this from poisonous mushrooms of similar appearance, and decided to stick to *pfifferlinge* as the only edible mushroom they would hunt for in the woods and later dare to eat. That was probably lucky for me.

If one goes to Germany in the summertime, *pfifferlinge* are sold in quantity in the supermarkets. At our local market they are available on occasion and are quite expensive, as I point out to Jeanette as we pass them in the supermarket. But I no longer eat *pfifferlinge*. Jeanette has read the story of Babar the Elephant: his uncle Cornelius picks mushrooms, eats a poisonous one, turns green, and dies. Jeanette never ate *pfifferlinge* when she came to Maine. After Karl and Ilse died, she said she was not comfortable nor happy that I picked and ate them. I was pleased to have a wife who was so attached to me that she could not tolerate the least risk of losing me. As I had been picking these chanterelles for over forty years, I thought the risk was negligible. But I had no interest in stressing my wife by eating the few mushrooms I picked. I promised to stop eating them. It was not a difficult thing to give up. But when my friends Jon and Eugenie Shaw came to Maine, I happened to find quite a few chanterelles one day. Eugenie is Norwegian and was quite familiar with them. She took a great many back to Sandwich, Massachusetts, and called to say that they were delicious.

CHAPTER 8:

My Mother Helps Me Get
Accepted at Friends Seminary

In 1951 I was about to graduate from public school and needed to find a high school to go to. I thought I would go to the Bronx High School of Science, or to Stuyvesant High School where my cousins, Peter and Albert, were going. I was good at math and did not think I would have trouble passing the entrance exam. Karl and Ilse had heard about Friends Seminary and scheduled me to have an interview with the principal, Mr. Alexander Prinz. My mother and I went down to 17th Street and met with the principal. I do not recall being asked anything unusual. My mother asked if the kids at that school read many books, and was assured that they did. After we left, I recall saying to my mother that the interview went well but we could not be sure I would get accepted. "You will be accepted," she said.

"How can you be so sure?" I asked.

"Mr. Prinz liked my hat," she said. At the time this response made no sense to me. Some years later, when I knew

Mr. Prinz better, I thought about my mother's remark and decided she had been quite perceptive and that her assessment as to whether and why the interview had been successful was probably absolutely on target.

Two or three days after my interview with Mr. Prinz, I came home and was told I had been accepted at Friends. I was still not sure I wanted to go. I asked my parents if they could afford the tuition. They said they could and that that was none of my business. (Tuition for ninth grade at Friends for the school year 1951-1952 was $400.) I asked, "Why should I go to Friends?" They said that at Bronx Science I might get beaten up—whereupon I said O.K. (Years later, the Chairman of the Department of Medicine at the Columbia Presbyterian Medical Center was reputed to be a very demanding and "tough" boss. I asked where he had studied and was told, "He went to high school at Bronx Science." I wondered if I would get beaten up by a Bronx Science kid after all.)

CHAPTER 9:

Students at the Berlin Girls' *Humanistisches* (Humanistic) Gymnasium Learned French, English, Latin, German, and Greek

When I was in high school I chose to take Latin rather than French, and my parents did not dissuade me. My folks approved of learning Latin, and thought classical languages were part of a general education. Both Ilse and Karl had studied Latin and some Greek. They knew French, and had I studied it they could have helped make me become fluent in conversational French; but I explained to them that I already knew German and getting involved with two European languages was more than I wanted. I knew I had to be "American" and find my way; my mother understood and did not encourage me to learn French.

In the summer of 1958, I was twenty and Kathy was ten, and we went with Karl and Ilse on a trip through Europe. I was the chauffeur; we bought a new Citroën, an ID-19 in Paris, a new model luxury sedan which I drove through France, Germany, and Spain. The car boasted a front engine and front-wheel drive, with a self-leveling suspension which depended on a hydraulic system and some "liquide" (fluid or oil) that kept the car afloat. We would sell the car back to the dealer when we returned to Paris. Our trip lasted six or seven weeks. It was an intense exposure to each other and our last major communal family endeavor. We were in Strasbourg looking at the cathedral one day and a young woman, probably a teenager, said in German to her friend, "Schau dir mal an diese komische Amerikanische familie" (Just look at that funny-looking American family). My mother heard her, turned around, and in her most vulgar and aggressive, colloquial Berlin German said, "Eine fresche unverschaemte dumme Ganz" (shameless, or perhaps better translated as "snotty," stupid goose). The girl was surprised and then said something else in French that was also derogatory. My mother then switched into French and insulted her further. By then the young woman understood she had made a mistake, shrugged her shoulders and laughed, as did we all, and ran away.

On the trip to Spain in 1958, we spent two weeks on the Costa Brava, staying at a new hotel which was in the luxury class but very inexpensive by American standards. The town was Lloret de Mar. In the afternoons Karl and I would go for a walk and sit in a local cafe and each of us would drink a beer. One day we walked in the hills behind the hotel where there were vineyards, and the vines were loaded with ripe grapes. My mother was happy to see all the grapes and picked some and ate them. I told her to be careful as there were federal police, the Guardia Civil, wearing uniforms and tricornered hats and carrying machine guns, and they patrolled these towns and vineyards and stood at the entrance and exit of each town, usually in pairs. "I don't want to get arrested for stealing grapes," I said. Ilse was not disconcerted in the least. She explained to me that picking grapes and putting them into a bag to carry them away is stealing, but picking grapes to put into one's mouth is simply a form of appreciating the surroundings and the landscape. She continued to pick a few grapes here and there and, sure enough, I soon saw a member of the Guardia Civil watching her. As we passed him some minutes later he smiled at us. I was not comfortable. Ilse smiled back.

CHAPTER 10

A Harvard Education and
a Course in Organic Chemistry
Pay Off on a Spanish Beach

In Spain we went to the beach one day. We were on the coast somewhere below Alicante. As we were leaving the beach, Karl was sitting on the sand looking at the soles of his feet, which were full of tar he had picked up while walking on the beach. He looked miserable and helpless. Nothing upset Ilse more than Karl's being helpless, and it was her personal mission in life to manage his episodes of neediness, misery, and helplessness. She would get irritable and unpleasant when Karl was helpless. My mother turned to me and said, "We sent you to Harvard for an education. Figure out how we can get that tar off Karl's feet." I remember answering that we were in the middle of nowhere; how should I find something to remove the tar? Then I had an idea. In those days gas stations were few and far between in Spain. Therefore, every driver had a canister of gasoline in the trunk of the car. We traveled with a five (or perhaps it was ten) gallon canister full of gasoline in the trunk. I went to the car and found the canister and a rag, and Karl discovered the tar could be removed quite easily by rubbing his feet with a rag soaked with gasoline. Karl was happy, Ilse was pleased he was no longer miserable, and I was pleased with myself. I pushed my luck when I praised myself by saying to my mother that I thought that was a clever idea to use the gasoline to remove the tar. She barked back (possibly there was a latent apology, although well-disguised or even hidden, in this for her having been so unpleasant when Karl was befuddled by the tar on his feet): "It was indeed a good idea, but it should not have been necessary for me to be so assertive before you got the idea. You should have been able to think of that without any prodding from me." Sometimes you cannot win.

My Mother Has Regrets When Karl's Dietary Restrictions Disappear

Ilse was very loyal to Karl and his work, and the success of her marriage to him was the most important thing in her life. Her children were important, but came second. When I was accepted at Harvard Medical School, my mother said it was good I would be living away from New York; being around someone studying a profession is intrusive on others, and the student is usually unaware that others do not want exposure to all that he is learning. Karl did not need such intrusion on his artistic interests. Such devotion for Karl's needs came in other forms. For many years Ilse carefully prepared foods, as Karl had a delicate stomach. He had diverticulosis, it turned out, and so was advised to avoid uncooked fruits and certain other items, including lettuce. For many years, and on the advice of Dr. Milton Rosenbluth (whose advice came with long, elaborate lists of appropriate foods to eat and/or avoid, which my mother carefully saved), Ilse always served Karl stewed fruit. (Dr. Rosenbluth was an

NYU professor and close friend of Karl's uncle, Dr. Marion Sulzberger, the Chief of Dermatology at NYU.) My mother spent many hours cooking peaches and pears for Karl. When Karl came to our house for supper in the 1980s and 1990s, Jeanette always served him avocado when others had a salad. Ilse took the care of Karl's food intake as a serious responsibility. She also thought he was quite helpless, and said to me on several occasions that if the poor man is cold at night in bed he can neither figure out that he should get another blanket nor that he should get up and close the window. "I need to do that for him," she would say. "He would never think of doing either and would be cold all night."

When in the late 1980s Karl needed to have surgery for colonic diverticulitis, Ilse went with him to see the doctor for a post-surgery follow up. "What should I give him to eat and what are the restrictions?" my mother asked. The surgeon, who was pleased he had cured Karl, said there were no food restrictions; Karl could eat whatever he wanted to eat. My mother was incredulous. For years she had been very careful to adhere to a special diet. She was almost disappointed that Karl could eat whatever he wished; it was as though she no longer was needed and that one of her main purposes in life had been taken away from her. The surgeon, who was rightfully well-pleased with himself (as most surgeons are on follow-up visits after the patient has been cured because of their surgical skill), was not aware that he had surgically excised not only the area of diverticulitis in Karl's colon but also some of my mother's *raison d'être*, as the French would put it.

Ilse was so loyal to Karl and to his work that I cannot recall her ever expressing any doubts about it. She liked his prints, his paintings, his drawings, and his watercolors. The closest she ever came to making a criticism was one day when she was making up a bouquet of flowers. I said they were lovely but that she seemed to be in a hurry. "What is the hurry?" I asked. She said, "I want to put this into the studio quickly before he gets started on another self-portrait." I laughed and said that there were never enough self-portraits, and that Rembrandt never tired of making them.

CHAPTER 12:

My Mother the Hitchhiker, and Her Puritanical Son

When I was four years old, we lived in Jackson Heights at 35-35 75th Street in a two-bedroom apartment. My grandmother had one bedroom, and my mother and I shared the other bedroom. My mother had a job working in a greenhouse in Flushing, Queens. I never really knew how she got to work in 1942 and presumed she took a bus. Many years later, she told me she would stand on Northern Boulevard and get a ride by hitchhiking. "The men were sometimes a bit aggressive," she would add. I only heard of this when she was in her eighties. At the time she did this hitchhiking she was thirty-two and an attractive woman, and I believe she got rides easily. There were gas shortages in 1942. My mother's sister was pleased that her husband, a medical doctor, had an extra allowance to buy gas, which was tightly rationed, and getting and giving rides was more common when those gas rationing restrictions limited the number of cars on the road. But even so, hitchhiking on Northern Boulevard does not seem like such a great idea. I was not shocked when I learned she had done this, but I, like most boys or men, prefer a more puritanical image or version of my mother; the idea that she was hitchhiking on Northern Boulevard was not really welcome.

I have become less puritanical about people and their personal lives than I once was. I remember a party given by Karl and Ilse shortly after they moved into the brownstone on East 95th Street. It was a formal party; the men wore tuxedos and the women wore evening gowns. My job at age ten or eleven was to greet people at the door and then take their coats upstairs or hang them on a rack in the hallway. (If my mother had had her way, this would still have been my job when they gave a big family party decades later.) After several guests had arrived, my mother came down wearing an elegant evening dress. It was very *décolleté*, low-cut and revealing, and my mother was well-endowed with a full figure. I thought this dress was too revealing and indecent, and found it hard to accept that this was my mother with breasts bursting out of her dress. So I stopped opening the door and receiving guests, sat on the stairs and cried, and was soon told I could go up to bed.

CHAPTER 13:

Some Memories of
My Mother from My Childhood

I was put into kindergarden at age four, but did not like it. I complained and said all we did was sing Christmas carols, and my mother said I need not go any more. I spent time with my grandmother, and then with a woman who lived in Kew Gardens with her husband, a Kaethe Schirokauer, later changed to Shearer. She and her husband Henry and their son Eric had lived in Cologne, Germany, where they had been patients of Dr. Ernst Brunell, the husband of my mother's sister Susie. Ernst recommended them to my working mother, and they cared for me if my grandmother was indisposed, which was most of the time. A year later, shortly after I turned five, the Shearers moved to Island Park. This was too far to commute there daily, so I started to live with them during the week and would spend the weekends with my mother or at my grandmother's or with my cousins in Jackson Heights. This continued until I was nine years old.

One winter day when I was four I went sledding with my

cousins. My mother put me on a sled and was about to push me off down the hill. My cousin Albert spoke up and said I was too little to go down that hill by myself. He said I would run right into a tree and bump my head. My mother did not agree and sent me off down the hill by myself. I headed right for the tree at the bottom and bumped my head. Fortunately, I was not going too fast and, although I cried, I was not badly hurt. Albert was always loyal and a good friend. We had an unusual bond; he was his mother's only son and I was my mother's only son, and our two mothers were sisters. The two sisters were similar in that they both were controlling of their sons, or tried to be, and were very attached to them in a way that was possessive at times. Their possessive love was sometimes a nuisance to us rather than a help. Only Albert and I knew what it meant to be the only son of Susie or Ilse. He and I stayed close all our lives. If someone had accused me of molesting a patient or robbing a bank, my cousin Albert would have unhesitatingly said, "No way." Other people close to me might have said, "Perhaps Peter was having a bad day," but Albert would have always insisted I was a decent person and that they were accusing the wrong person.

There was only one belief about me in regard to which Albert was dead wrong; I interpret his faith that I would be "good as a derivatives trader" as a sign of his high regard for me and his eagerness to teach me what he had mastered. Albert believed I had potential as a derivatives trader. No one else in the world imagined such a thing. When I mentioned this to my daughter-in-law Kirstin, a managing director of Bank of America, she laughed a good-natured laugh but did not think much of the idea. I never pursued this or even considered such an involvement, but simply took the suggestion as a sign of Albert's affection and good will. The other bond between me and Albert was that any medical problem or event affecting him was brought to my attention for comment or suggestions. Unfortunately, over the years there were quite a few problems, all of which were mastered or overcome except for his final incurable illness.

When I was five I went on vacation with my mother to Fleischman's in the Catskills. Jewish-German refugees frequented the place. My mother was single, a divorcée, and a good-looking thirty-three-year-old woman, and I found myself alone with other little kids under the care of someone the hotel provided. My mother was off on a hike for the day into the mountains. That was not to my liking, as I had little interest in the other kids; I had been promised a vacation and that I would spend time with my mother. I also recall that children were not allowed to have breakfast in the "adult" main dining room. Children had breakfast in a special room, under the supervision of someone who would relieve the parents from having to be involved with their kids at breakfast. I think that was a "Germanic" benefit provided by the hotel for its guests. I made a fuss. I said I would not eat at all unless I could eat with my mother. The hotel personnel said having little kids in the main dining room at breakfast was against the rules and was disturbing to the other guests. My mother explained she would have to leave, as I had been promised I would be with her, and the management relented. For the rest of our stay my mother and I had very pleasant breakfasts together in the main dinning room.

I started school at age five in September 1943 in the Island Park Public School, and went there from first through fourth grade. My name then was Peter Price, and my mother was Ilse Price. My mother had been very direct and forthright about explaining to me that she and my father had divorced, that he was in the French Foreign Legion or the British Army (actually he was first in the former and later in the latter), and that he would not come back. I knew he was a doctor. I secretly hoped he might return, but no one encouraged me to believe that would actually happen. Although not encouraged and even discouraged from believing he might come back, I still hoped he might show up. When teachers asked about my father, I did not mention any divorce but said he was in the war, in the army, and the teachers in my elementary school did not ask further questions. It was not so unusual to be a kid with a father in the army in 1943-1945, and the teachers were always sympathetic. I knew there were unasked and unanswered questions, but kept that to myself.

Commuting back and forth between New York City and Island Park on weekends was not complicated. Henry Shearer went to work in Manhattan on most Saturdays, so he often took me to Pennsylvania Station where my mother would meet us at the information booth near where the Long Island Railroad tickets were sold. To return on Sunday afternoon from Jackson Heights was also quite simple. My mother would take me to the Woodside Station of the Long Island Railroad, which is no great distance by the number 7 elevated train from Jackson Heights. I would take the train from Woodside station by myself to Island Park. I remember my mother asking the conductor, when I was five, to make sure I got off at Island Park. He knew me from previous trips and said to my mother, "He knows the stops and can call them out better than I can." Traveling alone as a child in 1943 on the Long Island Railroad was not dangerous, and going from the Island Park station to the Shearers' house was a short walk. Island Park was perfectly safe in those days.

CHAPTER 14:

Suzanne Fuchs Schrag and
My Mother

When my mother finished at the local "gymnasium" in Berlin, she spent a year at Heidelberg. There she met a girl/woman her own age, Suzanne Fuchs, who was born and lived in Strasbourg. They went swimming together and played tennis together, and became friends. Suzanne Fuchs would be a lifelong friend of my mother's (seventy years—from 1927, when they first met, until November 1997, when Ilse died). Suzanne Fuchs married Paul Schrag, emigrated with him to New York City, and reconnected with her friend Ilse in New York, where they both worked for Self Help in the late 1930s and early 1940s. (Self Help is a refugee support organization that exists to this day.) Susie invited her friend Ilse to her house for supper in 1939 and introduced Ilse to her brother-in-law Karl. In 1943 and 1944, she also placed her children, Francis and Eddy, with Mrs. Shearer in the summertime while she and Paul, Karl, and Ilse vacationed in Gloucester, Massachusetts with their friends, the artists James Brooks and Fred and Dorothy Farr.

Susie was to play an important role in my mother's life for the next fifty years, as both sister-in-law and friend. Karl and Ilse saw Paul and Susie almost weekly in the summer and wintertime, celebrated every New Year's Eve together, and lived near each other in Maine in the summertime. After driving up from New York City to Maine in separate cars on the same June day, they would meet at Jed Prouty's Tavern in Bucksport for dinner. They encouraged their children to be close friends. The relationship between Susie and Ilse was complicated in many ways, but that Susie had known Karl for many years as her bachelor brother-in-law and then later had to share him with Ilse was one of the problems. For several years, when Paul and Susie lived in Brussels in the years 1935-1938, Karl lived near them and saw them regularly. After Francis Schrag was born, Susie was a bit depressed and two weeks of skiing in the Alps was recommended. Paul could not leave his work, so Karl and Susie went off to Switzerland for two weeks of skiing. Susie was perfectly aware after 1945 that Ilse was Karl's wife, and acknowledged Ilse's status and importance, but never quite relinquished her priority with Karl. In Susie's old age (her early nineties) she once told me she introduced two of her brother-in-laws to their wives and said: "I made a mistake in both cases." I said Karl's marriage to Ilse lasted over fifty years and Fred Schrag's marriage to Ruth lasted over sixty years, so I doubted either had been a mistake.

But Susie was tough. Perhaps she felt a bit sorry for herself, as she was a widow by then, and was annoyed and disappointed that she was alone much of the time and saw less of Karl and Ilse than she had hoped she would. In a sense, some disappointment or unfulfilled expectations of Ilse that her sister-in-law expressed was a bit of a problem all the fifty years Ilse was married to Karl (from 1945 to 1995); the Schrags were close friends of my mother, but never fully or truly appreciated Ilse for her intelligence and her charm. They thought Ilse was too impulsive and were more inclined to laugh at her comments than to take them seriously. Ilse, in turn, was usually careful to admire Paul and Susie, their interest in good food and the arts and their refined manners, and accepted that being a Schrag was a special privilege. But she did not subscribe to this concept quite as totally as did those who were born Schrag. Karl said to me on several occasions that "the best fellowship is the Schrag Fellowship," by which he meant that to be free and independent and be a Schrag was indeed a privilege. Implicit too was the idea that there is no really good reason or need to hope for or ask for more.

Only rarely was Ilse really uninhibited in the presence of Paul and Susie. Ilse understood that, as Karl's wife, the most important role she played was to admire and support Karl and to keep him in the limelight, and not to upstage or divert attention from him. Ilse had her own ideas but often kept them to herself, in deference to Karl. I more than other family members understood and appreciated that my mother was highly intelligent, and I knew she was smarter than others realized. Even Karl, her husband, did not fully appreciate his wife, as he was self-centered. I think Karl's egocentricity was related mainly to his being an artist and being much of the time totally focused on lines, shapes, colors, and subjects represented in his art work. These were matters and considerations for which most other people had relatively little understanding. But Ilse understood Karl, and she knew and accepted that artists need to be self-absorbed in their creative efforts and need to be protected from unnecessary burdens or demands. She would have totally understood the housekeeper of Marcel Proust, who stayed up to unlock the front door for

Proust when he came home in the early morning hours rather than ask him to carry a key when he went out so he could later let himself back into his home. (See Monsieur Proust by Celeste Albaret, *New York Review of Books*, copyright 1973 & 2001, page 120.)

In the years 1995-1997, when they were both widows, Susie came to visit Ilse once a week without fail. They were exactly the same age, with birthdays three days apart (Ilse's was December 2, and Susie's was November 29, 1910), and these two women ate supper prepared by Barbara, Ilse's homemaker/home care attendant, every Wednesday evening. Susie said she was coming to care and look after Ilse. But I could not distinguish who was looking after whom, nor was it necessary to clarify which of these two sisters-in-law was more dependent on the other. After a dinner with good wine, dessert, and coffee, they would play cards. Then Susie would go home, always alone and unassisted, which was a point of pride with her.

For many years they had annoyed each other by complaining of each other's physique and eating habits: Ilse was too heavy, and ate too much and too quickly, and enjoyed eating too much for Susie's taste; Ilse thought Susie was too thin and underweight and too fastidious an eater. But these attitudes and critiques stopped once Paul and Karl were dead. These opposing attitudes were misinterpreted by people as personal criticisms of one another, but what was much more obvious after both women were widows was that these approaches to food and eating represented something else: these two women were advocating different policies as to how their husbands should be attended to. The controversy was a fierce policy difference and a reflection of the different styles they used to please or care for their husbands, rather than being a personal criticism of the other. I suspect many of my relatives would dispute my interpretation, but I think that, as these issues virtually disappeared after the husbands were dead, I am essentially right in my interpretation.

There was another aspect to Ilse not being quite fully appreciated as the perfect companion and support system for Karl. Ilse worried that Karl might outlive her, and that after she was dead Karl would fare well with a homemaker/care-taker, and that someone might say something to the effect that Karl never looked so well or had never been taken care of so well as now after Ilse was gone. They—and this "they" refers to hypothetical rather than actual people—were people my mother imagined and perhaps also feared, as "they" might say Karl was better off without Ilse, either because they thought it was true or because they disagreed with what they perceived as Ilse's manner of dealing with her husband, or because they were envious or did not understand or like my mother, and/or enjoyed being plain "mean." My mother would not have liked for Karl to be deemed to be flourishing better without her than with her, as she had devoted herself to Karl's welfare, making his life better than what he could have achieved alone. As Ilse was two years older than Karl, there had been a definite possibility that he would outlive her. What happened, however, was that Karl died in December of 1995 and Ilse survived him. She went through a terrible time after Karl died, and missed the man to whom she had been married for over fifty years. But I do not doubt that there was some consolation and gratification for her to know that Karl's life was defined by her life with him, and that no "better life" for Karl without her would or could exist.

Only very late in their life together did I once venture to criticize Karl. The issue had been whether my mother needed more help to run her household. He had adamantly insisted that more help would lead only to greater dependency, and was firmly opposed to getting his eighty-four-year-old wife more help. When I suggested to my mother that on this particular point Karl might be wrong, she shot back, "You stay out of my marriage, and I will stay out of yours." I backed off. By then Karl and Ilse had been married close to fifty years and nobody could tell them what to do.

CHAPTER 15:

My Mother's Chauffeur: Her Son

During the last four or five years of Karl's life, I often picked up my mother on Saturday mornings and drove her through town. This gave Karl and Ilse each a little time without the other, and my mother loved to be driven around town. I often took her to a farmer's market, where she enjoyed looking at fresh farm produce and would discuss seasonal growing problems and their use of insecticides with the farmers. Often she did some shopping for the dinner party she planned to have on Saturday night. Karl loved to give dinner parties for his friends and my mother was glad she could still do this. My driving her around town helped. My mother was a good cook and could have taught me to cook, but she never did. She said I should use my brains for something else. It was the only evidence I ever had that she had some regret or reservation about the work she did. So as not to leave me totally incapable of taking care of myself, my mother wrote out a series of simple recipes in a small booklet, which I still have. The purpose was to be able to maintain myself. I never was proficient enough at making meals to cook for other people except my children, which I did in the 1980s or, in more recent years, if Jeanette was sick, which fortunately (both for her and for myself) has happened very rarely.

Often my mother and I went to the greenhouses on Second Avenue above 100th Street and my mother would buy plants for her garden. She was a professional horticulturist and liked to discuss what I consider the subtle aspects of gardening with the greenhouse manager. She and he would exchange views as to when it was best to prune, when to plant certain bulbs, whether to leave the bulbs outside or bring them inside and store them in the basement of her house in the winter time, and how much to water certain plants. There was mutual showmanship, and sometimes she or the owner, who most often was Greek, knew something the other did not know. Late in her life my mother also was a little depressed and there was some paranoid ideation. One day I parked the car at a meter and returned to stand behind her as she withdrew some money from the ATM at the bank. She told me to back away. I asked if she worried that I might steal her PIN number and then her money. She nodded. I said I did not need to steal her money; I just had to wait a few years and I would get half of it anyway. I wondered if she would get angry but she smiled and said, "You know, you are right."

Once when we were shopping she hesitated as to whether she really wanted the item she had chosen, and the man at the checkout counter then kept her waiting as he did something else. Ilse was annoyed to be kept waiting and said, pointing to me, standing a few feet behind her, "I am here with my chauffeur, I pay him by the hour, and I am losing a fortune while you keep me waiting. I cannot afford this." I laughed but the man returned to serve her promptly.

CHAPTER 16:

From Studying Physics with Gertrude, Her Cousin, in Freiburg to Studying Horticulture and Being Kissed by Paul von Hindenburg

In 1929 my mother studied at the University of Freiburg, as did her cousin Gertrude Scharff. Gertrude was the elder daughter of Otto and Nellie Scharff, Otto being the younger brother of Ilse's mother. Ilse and Gertrude were friends and close since infancy, according to my uncle Henry Samton who said to me once, "You have no idea how close we were, Trude, her sister Lisselotte, and us; we were brought up like siblings." Gertrude was born in July 1911 and was seven months younger than my mother. Both studied physics at Freiburg at age nineteen. Late in her life my mother said, "I would have been a fairly good physicist but Trude was a great physicist and could solve the problems faster and more easily than I could, and I got discouraged." During that time they saw each other daily, ate supper together, and became close friends. They went skiing on weekends and joined a Jewish Socialist Youth Movement. The purpose of this organization, and the purpose of being a Socialist, was to try to steer the institutions of Germany between the hard right (the totalitarians and fascists) and the hard left (the communists). This was not a minor point in the Germany of the early 1930s, as fascists and communists were fighting in the streets of many cities. Both Jews and non-Jews would have to choose between loyalty to the right or the left in the decade that followed, as the events of European politics and German nationalism gradually evolved into World War II.

The time at Freiburg was to radically alter my mother's life; she injured her right knee on a skiing trip one weekend, needed surgery, was told it would be successful, and when she could not walk even seven weeks after the operation, had an emotional breakdown. She quit university life, remained depressed, and spent six months in a mental health facility which was a kind of sanitarium. Her cousin Trude sent me a letter years later telling me of the severity of Ilse's problems, which sounded like a psychotic breakdown with schizophrenic features. Ilse recovered after six months in the sanitarium. She decided to switch from physics and university life to horticulture and art. She thought of going to Palestine to make the desert bloom, and horticulture might help with that. Before her breakdown she had been introduced to Dr. Hans Preiss, a young doctor who was six years older than she was.

After she recovered and was released from the hospital, my mother worked in a greenhouse. One day Paul Ludwig Hans Anton von Beneckendorff und von Hindenburg, known as Paul von Hindenburg, the president of Germany at the time, visited the greenhouse and was introduced to my mother. My mother said he kissed her and shook her hand and said what a pleasure it was to meet such a lovely and charming German young lady. I would tease my mother, as Hindenburg was in his eighties by then; some had said he was already senile, and that he would even sign toilet paper if one presented it to him. So his judgment was perhaps suspect. Mentioning that Hindenburg's judgment may have been impaired annoyed my mother, so only once did I remind her of his possibly having already been senile. Thereafter I would say, slightly more diplomatically, that it was too bad that after showing such good judgment in regard to my mother, he then some months later appointed Adolf Hitler to be the Chancellor of Germany.

Years later, about the year 2000, my son Jonathan went from Vera Cruz, Mexico to Cuba with medical missionaries. They were bringing medical supplies, and as they got off the plane Fidel Castro himself was there to welcome and greet them and gave each person on that plane a kiss. So having kissed my mother on the cheek that Von Hindenburg had kissed, I now kissed my son on the cheek that Fidel Castro had kissed. The trick is to participate in historically interesting events and be greeted by famous people, but my preference is to be involved only indirectly.

CHAPTER 17:

The Goldhabers, Madame Wu, and My Mother

I lse's cousin Gertrude went on to get a Ph.D. *summa cum laude* from the University of Munich in Physics/Quantum Mechanics in 1935, at the age of twenty-four. Her son Alfred (Freddie) Goldhaber, speaking at his mother's funeral in 1998, said that when his mother congratulated him on getting his Ph.D. in physics from Princeton University at age twenty-five, she added, "Of course I was twenty-four when I got my Ph.D. in physics." Gertrude met Maurice Goldhaber at the University of Berlin, where they both studied physics and later went on to have careers as prominent physicists at Brookhaven National Laboratories on Long Island. The Goldhabers had no other family on the East Coast and came to our family Thanksgivings from about 1950 to 1980. Karl, Ilse, Kathy and I visited them at their home in Bayport, Long Island, once or twice combining a visit to them with a day or two on nearby Fire Island. When my mother was seventy-five, we had a small gathering at Karl and Ilse's home and

Trude came in from Bayport for the occasion. Trude and my mother were lifelong close friends.

The Goldhabers came often to Boston when I was a student there, from 1955 to 1964. They had personal and professional dealings with the physics communities both at Harvard and M.I.T. They always included me for a lunch or supper with their friends or family. I was interested in math and physics then, and we discussed people, courses, and problems in physics and math. I have an undergraduate degree in mathematics (cum laude) from Harvard College. I think they were disappointed when I told them I was going to go to medical school rather than study mathematics or physics. When I lived on Hammond Street (from 1962 to 1964) they came over for breakfast on occasion; it was a short walk from the Hotel Commander where they stayed. I saw Trude in 1963 when I was a third-year medical student and when Michael was hospitalized with a pneumothorax. She quizzed me about this medical condition, which is more likely to happen to people with asthma, which is what Michael had. I recall that I once saw Trude in Boston when I was a student there and she asked how my grandmother, who was Trude's aunt, was managing. I mentioned that my by-then elderly grandmother had recently fallen, but was O.K. Trude remarked casually that my grandmother had always had a tendency to fall; even as a young woman she had fallen occasionally, according to Trude. This was something I could not corroborate from my experience. I mentioned this to my mother. Ilse was annoyed and said, for the only time in her life as far as I can tell, something critical of her cousin: "Trude is a bit too tough."

In 1956 I was a sophomore at Harvard College. That spring vacation, Trude called and invited me to come out to Brookhaven National Laboratories to be shown around and to stay with them for the weekend at their home in Bayport. At the time Maurice was not only a senior physicist at

Brookhaven but also was the Director of Brookhaven. The real purpose of the visit was to tell Fred (Alfred Scharff Goldhaber), their elder son, and Michael Goldhaber, their younger son, who were respectively two and four years younger than me, about Harvard. Trude had the idea that I might be helpful to her sons, just as she and my mother had been helpful to one another in the 1930s at the University of Freiburg. I knew both Fred and Michael as we had celebrated Thanksgiving together for some years and did not mind being asked to go out there, but as I had other plans with friends, I tried to get out of going. This did not sit well with my mother. She said then, and I remember it well, "Maurice and Trude can hold their own with the world's greatest scientists. Any interest they take in you and/or your career will only be to your advantage. They may make demands on you, they may test your knowledge, skill, and abilities to the very utmost, but they will never involve you in anything without there being something in it for you. That's how they do business." So I went out to Brookhaven and was shown around by Fred and Michael, and for a while also by Trude and Maurice.

In 1956, T.D. Lee of Columbia University and C.N. Yang from Brookhaven were working at Brookhaven on whether parity was conserved. They would receive the Nobel Prize in Physics for their work in 1957. I remember meeting them and other physicists in the Brookhaven lunch room, which was quite a plain cafeteria with simple food and tables and chairs like any ordinary, low-priced, run-of-the-mill cafeteria. In Maurice's office there was a large photo of Albert Einstein hanging behind his desk. I greatly respected the Goldhabers and knew my mother respected and loved her cousin. But I also had a chance to see Trude reprimand a graduate student for some work that she thought needed to be redone and was surprised at how fierce and critical she could be. It was an interesting weekend, and I must have said some nice things about Harvard College as both Fred and Michael Goldhaber went there.

The Nobel laureates T.D. Lee and C.N. Yang had their work confirmed by another physicist, Madame Chien Shiung Wu, a physics professor at Columbia University, who was an expert on beta decay and who did experiments using Cobalt 60 at low temperatures that confirmed the theories of Lee and Yang. Madame Wu was a contemporary of my mother; my mother lived from 1910-1997 and Madame Wu lived from 1912-1997. Madame Wu was a very prominent physicist and was the first person to win the Wolf Prize in physics, in 1978. This prize is given by the Wolf Foundation in Israel. Maurice Goldhaber was the winner of the Wolf Prize in Physics in 1991. The award to Maurice was made in Israel at a session of the Knesset. My daughter and son-in-law were there at the time, and attended probably more as a favor to me than as a favor to Maurice. Friends and family who could not make it to Israel were invited to a reception at the Israeli Embassy in New York City which was scheduled to honor Maurice. I went and remember it well. When you are admitted to the Israeli Embassy, a door closes behind you and a door locks in front of you, you feel caged (and actually are), and then you are asked some questions before the doors are unlocked and you can proceed. It is a disquieting experience.

Maurice, Trude, my mother and Karl, Maurice's brother Gerson and his wife (Gerson was a professor of physics at the University of California at Berkeley), and I were all there, as was Madame Wu. My mother got into a long conversation with Madame Wu and suggested she might like to join the Women's City Club of New York. They seemed to enjoy talking to one another, and of course my mother identified herself to Madame Wu as Gertrude Goldhaber's cousin and friend. I overheard my mother saying to Madame Wu that she would have no difficulty getting admitted to the Women's

City Club (at which I smiled), and Madame Wu seemed genuinely interested. My mother later forwarded information about this club to Madame Wu who did, according to my mother, become a member. My mother liked being a "matchmaker."

My parents stayed friendly with an elderly, wealthy woman named Adele Scofield, who had been a close childhood and thereafter lifelong friend of Karl's mother. She was quite elderly when she came to tea one afternoon. She was lively and well-informed. My mother was impressed and asked her to what she attributed her lively mind and many interests and her youthful demeanor. Adele Scofield then said she kept young by going regularly to the Women's City Club. Not long after this my mother applied for membership in that club and was admitted on some basis. She attended meetings regularly for several decades. After her death, I received several letters from women who commented on some improvements my mother had suggested for their meetings. According to one of those letters, some of the recommendations she had made seem to have greatly improved the kind of dessert and coffee they served. I laughed as that seemed quite probable; my mother participated in things by giving some thought as to how they could be improved, then would speak up, and usually was correct. Improvements in the quality of food served was second nature to her. Unfortunately, I too seem to have learned to participate by making or suggesting changes. It must be in the genes.

CHAPTER 18:

May 19, 1951: My Bar Mitzvah Followed by a Family Luncheon

My cousins and I all had bar mitzvahs. Claude was the eldest, and his was at the Jewish Center in Jackson Heights, Queens. All my other cousins, the grandsons of my maternal grandmother, Peter and Albert, and the cousins on the Schrag side, Francis, Eddie, and Raymond Schrag, and I too had bar mitzvahs at Congregation Habonim (*habonim* means "the builders" in Hebrew). This was a congregation formed by German Jewish refugees and, in those days, was always closer to the reform than the conservative side of Judaism. The Rabbi was Hugo Hahn, and the cantor was Erwin Hirsh. Hirsh was my teacher during the three years Fran and I went to Hebrew School every Tuesday afternoon. He taught me to read Hebrew, worked with me on my Torah portion from Leviticus which I read in Hebrew from the Torah Scroll at my bar mitzvah, and taught us Jewish History. He was a good teacher, and he particularly liked the story of Esther in ancient Persia and told it well. (Even then, relations between Jews and non-Jews were by no means simple.) I also had a Haftorah portion which I was allowed to read in English rather than Hebrew which was customary at Congregation Habonim.

In 1951, when I had my bar mitzvah, the services were held in the True Sisters Building on West 84th Street between Amsterdam and Columbus Avenues, in a rented room on the second floor. A stage was at the front of the room. Just before the closing prayer for that Saturday service, Rabbi Hahn addressed me and presented me with a copy of a Bible (the Old Testament) with an inscription commemorating my bar mitzvah. I still have it on a bookshelf in my living room. Only in 1958 did Congregation Habonim have its own building, on West 66th Street. Rabbi Hahn and Cantor Hirsh held services in Forest Hills, Queens every other Saturday morning, and in Manhattan on the other Saturdays as the German Jewish population of Queens in Jackson Heights and Forest Hills was large in those days. For my bar mitzvah I wore a new light blue suit, a white silk yarmulke, and a shiny brand new tallis/prayer shawl. My parents, uncles, and aunts, Henry and Kaethe Shearer, and my friends attended. My cousins who had had their bar mitzvahs before me, Albert, Peter, Claude, and Francis, were called up to the Torah; each had an aliyah. Karl was not into being called up to the Torah because he could not have said the blessings as required in Hebrew. Ilse would have come up if the service were held today but, although girls had bat mitzvahs in 1951, women were not called up to the Torah yet except at bat mitzvahs at Congregation Habonim in 1951.

After the service we had lunch at 127 East 95th Street in the kitchen. I remember it was a party of nineteen people and Karl was pleased that his Uncle Nathan Sulzberger had also come. I stood up at one point and thanked everyone for coming. As I sat down I saw my mother was crying and her face was full of tears; she was happy and at that moment I did not doubt she and Karl loved me.

In 1955 I graduated from high school, as did my cousin Francis Schrag. Fran and I went to Europe that summer, visiting friends and relatives of our parents. We had lunch at my parents' house before leaving for the dock on the lower west side, where the *Groote Beer* (the large bear), a ship of the Holland America Line, was docked. This boat would take us and about three hundred students and some teachers to Rotterdam. It would take us ten days to cross the Atlantic Ocean. At lunch Susie Schrag and my mother warned us to be careful and we discussed being alert for pickpockets. As we got into the car to drive to the dock, Ilse asked Fran if he had his wallet. He did not. He was a bit upset for a few seconds, then she handed it to him. My mother had picked his pocket and he had had no idea that it had been done.

CHAPTER 19:

My Mother Protects Me from Her Cousin and Her Sister

In 1970, I went into medical practice and had an office on 90th Street. My mother's sister referred a patient to me, her cousin Else Abeles. I decided I did not want to get involved with Else Abeles. My aunt was offended. She said she was referring a wealthy patient to me who lived on Park Avenue and who would come to my office regularly as it was near to where Else Abeles lived. If I refused such a referral, my future success as a medical doctor was, according to my aunt, in severe jeopardy. However, there was a problem with Else Abeles that I did not want to get involved with; she was a morphine addict and this would not end well in my estimation. She had married a man named Mohr Abeles, who, according to my mother, had been the richest Jew in Frankfurt. This meant he was probably among the twelve richest Jews in Frankfurt, as Ilse tended to exaggerate financial matters, probably to get attention from her two older siblings who considered her ignorant about finances.

Else was the only child of Dagobert Szamatolski, Dagobert, Max, and Richard being the three brothers of my maternal grandfather, Albert Szamatolski. All of the brothers except for Dagobert remained Jewish. (Dagobert had made a fortune selling some liniment in the Balkans to the Bulgarians before the first World War. He became very rich. He then donated a railroad car that was to be a medical car for the wounded in the first world war. Around 1920 he wanted to go into politics but was told no Jews succeed in German politics, so he became a Protestant. Then he was continually asked on the political trail what had he been before he became a Protestant. This was annoying so he then became a Catholic. He could then answer, when asked what his previous religion had been, that previously he had been a Protestant.)

Mohr and Else's daughter was Anne-Marie, the one with the large Cadillac convertible who came to Long Beach to visit us there in 1944. Anne-Marie married several times, and at several of these weddings her mother's cousins, my aunt Susie and her husband who were close friends of Else and Mohr, were not invited as, allegedly and according to my aunt, Jews were excluded or unwelcome. I recall visiting my aunt and hearing her say to her cousin Else, "If we are not invited to the weddings, we will not come to the funerals." My aunt was always blunt and forthright and was certain that her cousin had wanted to exclude her Jewish relatives from Anne-Marie's weddings. (But the Good Lord has a sense of humor and stratagems of his own, and punished these Jews who turned from Him and rejected their religion; of all the descendants of the four Szamatolski brothers, none looked as stereotypically Jewish as did Else Abeles, who claimed she was not Jewish.) I believe my aunt and her husband, Dr. Ernst Brunell, did not attend the wedding of Anne-Marie, but nonetheless they stayed close with Else and Mohr. Their frequent get-togethers involved Susie and Mohr discussing investments and strategies for playing the stock market, while Ernst handled Else's needs for morphine shots. Susie referred to these get-togethers nostalgically after Mohr had died.

When I opened my office in 1970 my uncle, Dr. Ernst Brunell, had been dead for three years. Else Abeles needed a new and reliable provider of morphine injections. Using me was an attractive opportunity; as a child of Else's cousin Ilse and being susceptible to pressure from my aunt, Else (and my aunt) thought and hoped Else's supply of morphine might soon be assured and steady. My mother never saw this cousin socially (unless it was at some big family event), and I had never heard anything particularly redeeming from my mother about the Abeles family except for Mohr being "rich." I appealed to my mother to explain to her sister that I did not want to give morphine shots to Else Abeles and to leave me alone. Telling her sister that she was wrong was never a task that my mother liked, as it was never easy to do, but telling her sister to leave me alone, especially as Ilse agreed I should not have to service Else Abeles with morphine injections, was not a problem for my mother and she got Susie and Else Abeles off my back.

CHAPTER 20:

My Mother the Zionist, and Related Religious and Irreligious Sentiments

In her youth Ilse dreamt of going to Palestine and making the desert bloom and, therefore, studied horticulture in the early 1930s. In 1944 she belonged to the Zionist Organization of America and I still have the membership card. My daughter, who speaks Hebrew and is married to an Israeli/American and who is close with her husband's family in Israel, thought it silly of me to say her grandmother had been a Zionist: "Dad, Ilse was no Zionist." Deb was right in that, when she knew my mother, Ilse had adapted to Karl's life which included very little or rather no interest in Israel or much in the way of Jewish observance except for going to my bar mitzvah. Karl identified himself as an artist and an American. Karl never had any desire to visit Israel. Karl was one of four brothers, and all four—Otto, Fred, Paul, and Karl—married Jewish women. None of the four Schrag brothers had bar mitzvahs. Otto's second wife, Alice, was not Jewish. I never met Judith Haas, Otto's first wife. I knew

Fred's wife Ruth well. I knew Susie, Paul's wife, all my life. Karl's wife was, of course, my mother. Susie went to synagogue regularly. (Dr. Marion Sulzberger, Karl's uncle and the brother of Karl's mother, wrote some memoirs in which he mentions that his parents would light Sabbath candles on Friday nights. This came as a surprise to me, and was of interest as I had thought the Sulzbergers were not observant in any way. It was also a surprise to Karl.)

My mother said to me during one of the Arab-Israeli wars, "If Israel does not survive I will kill myself." That was not true and was simply a statement to say she was very upset with the possibility of Israel losing that war. One day I was walking with Karl and said that I knew he had never wanted to be identified primarily as a Jewish artist nor had he taken any great interest in "Jewish" affairs or Israel; did he have any regrets about this? He said he and my mother had had guests for supper at their house the other evening and had entertained their old friends Bernard Malamud and his wife Ann, Isaac Bashevis Singer and his wife Alma (Wassermann née Haimann), and Raphael Soyer and his wife Rebecca, whose home on Vinalhaven my parents had rented for two summers in the late 1950s. Karl said, "How much more Jewish can you get?" The point of mentioning this is that Karl's ethnic identity was not linked to any religious belief, learning, or observance, but was a cultural and social influence in his life. Ilse knew more than Karl about traditional Jewish life and religion. It was she who took me when I was a boy to her neighbors, Rabbi and Mrs. Langer, to see their succa on Succoth.

The Szamatolskis were highly assimilated Jews and were not very observant. But Jews who could "pass" in the non-Jewish world become, under unusual circumstances, an important resource to the Jewish community. Being able to travel without being recognized as Jewish is an aptitude that can be extremely helpful and useful; my mother's sister and her brother were both adept at transferring money from Germany to Holland when it was illegal and dangerous to do in the 1930s. My aunt did this for the benefit of many Jewish families for whom this was of critical importance. They appreciated the transferring of their financial assets to Holland and paid a commission.

My mother was aware that the assimilated German Jews were different from the observant Eastern Jews. She would on occasion, but rarely, use the term "Black Jews," a term I dislike and which refers to the more orthodox Jews. Much to my surprise I saw in the Book Review of the *New York Times* on July 3, 2016 a review of a book by the Israeli author, A.B. Yehoshua, in which it was stated that a neighborhood in Israel, formerly a bastion of secularism, had changed and the "Black Jews," the ultra-orthodox, had moved in. I had not given any thought to this term in years. I dislike it as much as I dislike the term "Jaeke," which my orthodox neighbors use as a term to designate German Jews who are punctual. The term comes from the word jacket (*jaeke* is jacket in yiddish) that assimilated Jews wore rather than the long Kaftans, i.e. black long coats worn by the more religious and less assimilated Jews. My neighbor Barney Koenigsberg, who is now eighty-six years old and with whom we have been friendly for over thirty years, said he uses the term "jaeke" all the time and that it is innocent, and he denied that the term "jaeke" is derogatory. But then he went on to elaborate that Sidney, the husband of our mutual friend Janine (née Langer, the daughter of Rabbi and Mrs. Langer), who died some years ago, was a real *jaeke*: "If one had been invited for 7:30 and came at 7:31 Sidney would go ballistic, he was a real *jaeke* and nobody really liked him."

My friend Mordecai Rosenfeld, a lawyer and graduate of Yale Law School and a friend and classmate at Yale Law School of the liberal politician and congressman Allard Lowenstein, who started the "dump Johnson" movement in

1968, says that without any question "jaeke" is derogatory, and I believe him. There is enough anti-semitism in the world, so I think Jews should not use derogatory terms when referring to a group or class of Jews. But the terms exist and are used. My mother disliked or perhaps feared the orthodox, and used the term "Black Jews" occasionally. She believed in a secular multi-ethnic society. Of my orthodox neighbors she said, "Maybe it's not so bad that they are observant and cannot eat in your home; that keeps you from running a kibbutz on the ninth floor." My mother would take offense if one assumed she liked gefilte fish. She regarded this as a Lithuanian dish which a certain class of people in Lithuania ate, and as so many people in Lithuania had been Jewish this food was associated in the minds of many with "being Jewish." My mother resented stereotypes that were simplistic or which might misrepresent a group.

When my mother met my first wife she was not thrilled that I was involved with the daughter of a conservative rabbi. She heard that my first wife's uncle was a rabbi in Jamaica, Queens, and went there to a service one Saturday to see how orthodox the service might be. Ilse tried to dissuade us from keeping a kosher home, which was of importance to my first wife's parents. Ilse was worried I would have to get involved with more rituals and observances than I needed or wanted to observe. When years later I had coffee at my parents' home, if we were alone, my mother would express her poorly concealed annoyance at our keeping Kosher by commenting, "It is good you take your coffee black, you could not take milk with your coffee in your own home after eating meat." But our slight tilt towards traditional religious customs and religious observance was not really the problem in my first marriage. More problematic was that my first wife inherited from her father a respect for observance of rules, a high regard for procedures and their importance, a desire to be a moral authority, an almost biblical preoccupation with righteousness and the punishment of evildoers, and a desire to be prominent, have status, be socially influential, and to associate and mingle with powerful people.

All of these ambitions and preoccupations could find their expression or be fulfilled by becoming a zealous prosecutor (and be further fulfilled by becoming, if at all possible, a judge). But living with what I now think of as "our homegrown prosecutor" was awful for me. So my mother's apprehension that I was possibly getting involved with more ritual and procedure than I needed or wanted or could tolerate was correct, but it was preoccupation with legal procedures, not religious rituals, that was intolerable. When in 1983 I told my mother that my divorce came through, she said, "You did all right, you raised four interesting children." I remember that Ilse and Karl thought Deborah might be too Jewish a name, and that Daniel and Jonathan were similarly looked upon as "very Jewish." Their generation wanted to protect children from discrimination; their concern was that these names might cause problems for the children.

Ilse and I differed on other important issues. Ilse thought I got married too young and for years afterwards gave away books I had had as a boy, saying, "If he is old enough to get married, he does not need these books any more." She also thought I had children when I was too young. But she and Karl did get attached to my children, and Karl always considered my children his grandchildren and stated explicitly in his will that my kids were to be treated as though they were his natural grandchildren. They saw Deb, Dan, and Jon regularly when they were students in New York City. When Daniel graduated from Yale, Karl and Ilse drove up with me to New Haven. They enjoyed the luncheon in the quadrangle of his "college" at Yale. They also visited Daniel in California when he was at Berkeley (in connection with a visit to Karl's brother and sister-in-law Fred and Ruth in San Francisco), and some years later, when Daniel was at Princeton, Karl and Ilse visited him there. Ilse noticed what were clearly some Jewish kids at Princeton and told me in the car on our return that she felt better about Princeton after having been there and seeing those kids.

My mother's religious belief approximated believing that anyone more observant than she was quite possibly a Chassid, and anyone less observant than she was quite possibly a Christian. But she did identify closely with being Jewish. She said to me on several occasions that just as one needs to add yeast to flour to make bread because baking bread without adding yeast to the flour results in uninteresting and tasteless bread, one needs Jews in a city as without Jews a city is dull, uninteresting, and without life. I was influenced by Ilse, yet I am probably more sympathetic to observant Jews than she was. But I certainly cannot claim to be observant, as I do not believe in prayer. That is not to deny that the ritual of blessings before wine or bread in Hebrew are pleasant rituals, or that the festival of Passover and the Seder is a happy family event, or that bar mitzvahs are meaningful for the family and the bar mitzvah boy.

My family and I, either directly or indirectly (i.e. I was not born in Europe and was never there before 1955), were all refugees from Nazi Germany. We unquestionably participated in the Jewish experience of the twentieth century. I have accepted that religion is not something one can ignore, even though one might like to. I believe religious conflict and discrimination are here to stay. It is ridiculous to imagine that I am anything but Jewish.

The tradition of secular Judaism to which I can relate should be neither denied nor underestimated; Israel was founded by secular Jews. The intellectual historian Isaiah Berlin, the son of a Russian Jewish timber merchant named

Mendel Berlin who immigrated from Russia to England in 1920, writes about the socialist Zionist Moses Hess, who is commemorated in Israel with streets in his name: "He believed in natural science applied to create social welfare; he believed in cooperatives, communal endeavor, state ownership, or, at any rate, public ownership. To a large degree, these principles have today been realized in the state of Israel. . . . The foundations of his beliefs, both Socialist and Zionist, were unashamedly moral. He was convinced as a matter of empirical knowledge, that moral beliefs played a major role in human affairs." ("The Life and Opinions of Moses Hess," in *Against the Current*, by Isaiah Berlin, pages 250 and 251, The Viking Press, 1980.) My mother, like Hess, was a believer in the importance of communal endeavors. Also of interest to me is that Moses Hess, although a collaborator with Karl Marx and Frederich Engels, did not believe in the rougher aspects of socialism, with class warfare and revolutionary rhetoric and upheavals, as did Marx and Engels. In fact, Berlin quotes Marx as referring to Hess as "that donkey Hess." But my mother would have liked Hess; she too believed in being positive, communal, constructive, scientific, and rational in one's approach to society. She thought one should not let oneself become preoccupied with economics, economic warfare, anti-semitism, crematoriums, and concentration camps. My mother believed in people's better nature, which included hope for a Germany that was less right-wing, more supportive of foreigners and of diversity, and not obsessed with vitriolic anti-semitism. Such optimistic hopes made others think of her as simple.

But perhaps "that donkey Hess" was wiser than Marx, and perhaps my mother can be excused for avoiding Holocaust museums. My mother believed that, to some degree, although it may only be to a very limited degree, one can help create the world one prefers to believe in. And even if one cannot shape the world in accordance with one's values, just supporting the values may do some good and contribute to thoughtfulness and enlightenment and help keep the philistines from getting away with still more nonsense.

CHAPTER 21:

Harrison Salisbury and My Mother Meet at the Women's City Club

The divorce from Hans Price exerted a permanent toll on my mother's life. In 1952 she explained to me she might not be able to vote for Adlai Stevenson for president. When I asked her why not, she answered, "I may not be able to vote for a man who has been divorced." But she later changed her mind and did vote for Stevenson rather than for Eisenhower. Another result of her divorce from Dr. Hans Preiss was that my mother did not like doctors, as I shall discuss in more detail below. She had some trouble reconciling herself to my being a doctor. But I do believe my mother eventually had some pleasure and pride from my being a doctor. This was thanks to the Women's City Club. My patient for over twenty years, Mr. Harrison Salisbury, an author and an editor of the *New York Times* who was very devoted to me and in whom I had put a cardiac pacemaker in 1975 (this was no secret; it was referred to at length in public at his memorial service), was scheduled to speak at the Women's City Club. He and my mother were in their eighties at the time, so it was perhaps in 1991 or 1992. My mother received an announcement of this talk and asked me if she could go up afterwards and introduce herself. I said she should do so by all means; Harrison liked me and would no doubt be pleased to meet her. So she went up to introduce herself to him at the end of his talk. He was gracious and told her how proud she must be of me and how much he appreciated what I had done for him. I heard from both Harrison and my mother that each was pleased to have met the other. All this occurred before 1993, when Harrison died at age eighty-six.

CHAPTER 22:

Knitting Sweaters for Me and Teaching Knitting in Harlem

My grandmother knew how to knit and crochet and did it much of the time. Her daughter Ilse also was a good knitter. As a boy I wore many sweaters that my mother had knitted. As I got bigger my mother would have trouble completing the sweater or would become impatient, so that usually one sleeve was not joined at the shoulder properly; there was a slight puff or bulge at the shoulder. I still have several of those sweaters and am no longer so vain as to be bothered by the irregular shoulder, but as a boy this bothered me as it seemed somewhat feminine to have a puffed sleeve at the shoulder. But many of the sweaters my mother knit for me were "tennis sweaters" to wear after playing tennis, and for these more bulky sweaters the bulge at one shoulder did not matter to me. In the 1970s my mother would go to Harlem and teach knitting to women. She did this for almost ten years and was well-liked, as she was a patient and cheerful teacher and the women soon learned to knit sweaters, hats, dresses, and scarves for their families. She went alone into Harlem and never worried as to whether she, a not-so-young white woman, would be unsafe. For some years when I was a boy, Susie Schrag and Ilse would work on the same knitting projects and Fran Schrag and I would have identical sweaters .

CHAPTER 23:

Abusive and Angry, but Indiscriminately So— or So I Maintain

When my mother was widowed in December of 1995 after being married to Karl for fifty and a half years, which was more than ten times as long as her first marriage had lasted, Kathy and I decided she could no longer live alone. Ilse objected, but I said she had trouble getting out of the bathtub and I did not want her to be found after being stuck helplessly in the bathtub for several days. So my eighty-five-year-old mother reluctantly agreed that she would have full-time help to assist her with cooking, laundry, bathing, and going out. But she was still quite angry and depressed. She said she would only have a caretaker in her home if she could participate in the interviews we would conduct to find someone.

We hired a social worker affiliated with Mt. Sinai Hospital, Naomi, who would find us people to interview. After over half a dozen interviews, Naomi came to me and said, "Dr. Schrag, your mother is an elderly German lady and she has been obnoxious to several black home care workers and has said offensive things to them. I think we should eliminate all the black home care workers and just interview white women." I told Naomi that I did not agree. Unquestionably my mother was abusive but I did not think she was a racist; she was just depressed, angry, and still unwilling or unable to accept a care provider without being highly critical and ambivalent. I thought she was indiscriminately abusive to workers quite irrespective of their particular background, and I had trouble convincing the social worker that this was so. I claimed that my mother would say something objectionable or find something objectionable or offensive to say to anyone until she found someone she could relate to. I told Naomi I did not want to eliminate a significant percentage of home care providers by restricting our search to non-black workers. I knew, which Naomi did not, that my mother had gone into Harlem to teach knitting for many years, had enjoyed being useful to that community, and was liked and respected. I did not bother to tell Naomi as she would not be convinced.

But after a few more interviews we found Barbara and Jennifer. These two women were black, and they cared for my mother for the last two years of her life. I cannot say that my mother behaved well to them at all times, but to describe their complicated relationship—the personalities of the two women, how my mother interacted with them, the number of Chinese restaurants Jennifer went to with my mother, the number of times they went to the beauty parlor and discussed hairdos or hair coloring or problems of family life, the tricks each of these home attendants used to control my mother if and when she was obstreperous, and when I would need to intervene—would require an entire book in itself. In the process I needed to deal with my sister and her suggestions, my mother and her objections, Jennifer and her complaints, and Barbara and her needs. I could not always tell who was making up stories about the other, sometimes true and sometimes imagined slights, and this occurred in all combinations. This was complicated for a while because my mother had some paranoid ideation when her depression got worse. In addition, some old friends would visit and then give me a follow-up call, which might include praise for how well I was keeping my mother but more often included dismay over some aspect of her condition, her dress, or something she said. I was occasionally tempted to say: "If you are so critical be careful; I might just ask you to take my mother home with you to your house and let you manage her." I never felt I needed more suggestions and input from friends in those days. There were also occasional surprises, such as an old good friend who repeatedly encouraged and urged Kathy to have Ilse put into a nursing home. This was not at all necessary and annoyed me as it was more of a nuisance than a help.

Twice Kathy and I thought our mother was having delusions only to discover that she had been quite right and we were wrong. She made what we thought was a ridiculous assertion that she could hear the phone conversations of her next door neighbors on her telephone. This we dismissed as obviously related to delusional paranoia. But then we too heard the neighbor's phone conversations. It turned out there was some problem with the wiring due to the phone company, rather than a problem due to my mother's state of mind. Around this time my mother called to say someone was shooting into the large plate glass window in Karl's studio and that some bullet holes were now in the glass. I dismissed this too as paranoia. That plate glass window had been there for decades and no one had ever shot into it. But when I inspected the window some three days after my mother had called, there were the bullet holes.

The damage was covered by insurance, but the insurance company required placing a police report and obtaining the number of the police report before paying for the damage. So I went to the police station and tried to file a report. The policeman at first refused to accept it saying I had waited too long; had I called right away they would have caught the offender, is what he claimed. I explained that my eighty-six-year-old, mildly paranoid mother lived alone and I, at first, had not believed her. I recall that the policeman enjoyed making the point that I was in the wrong and that my mother had been in the right. Ilse would have enjoyed listening to him. I was happy he finally took the report and authorized filing it so I could get a number for the insurance company. The glass was replaced and the expense was fully covered by the insurance.

My mother's "obnoxious" comments for which I would find excuses were unacceptable to my daughter. My daughter said to me that some of her grandmother's comments were openly racist and were totally unacceptable. My attitude is that there is a generational and cultural gap. What my mother's generation would do and what her grandchildren could not tolerate was to be outspoken, frank and insulting if it suited the situation, but racial or personal hatred was not part of it. I recall my former boss visiting us in Deer Isle with his family. He had a son in his twenties who was mentally retarded. After our guests had left my mother said "I enjoyed meeting your friend/boss and his idiot son." I winced. But there was no malice involved. My mother believed what many Germans believed: do not use euphemisms or gloss over the obvious. Not everyone appreciates this trait, and my children in particular objected to their grandmother's excessive forthrightness without deference to good manners or political correctness. Another element in these moments when offensive terms were used is simply that what is acceptable in language can change quickly and older people are "out of touch." As recently as this evening I was corrected and told that referring to "underdeveloped countries" or to "the underdeveloped world" is now totally unacceptable; the proper term now is "resource-deprived." My mother would not have bothered to stay current with such revisions. My mother certainly did not hesitate from calling her grandchildren too fat or bad mannered, or complaining of their poor posture.

Personal criticism was almost my mother's specialty, although Susie Schrag may have equaled my mother in this respect. This tendency not to hesitate to highlight what seemed to them obviously objectionable was, unfortunately, not just a trait of my mother's; I too developed a similar tendency to insist on not burying an unpleasant fact just because it is troublesome to confront or acknowledge. This worked out mostly to my advantage in North Carolina, where I was distressed about what was going on in the textile industry and spoke up. It did not work out when I could not overlook some sleazy practices among my medical colleagues and called them on their nonsense. My cousin Albert was a teenager when he called our grandmother's attention to her esteemed bridge partner. This was a woman my grandmother had been friends with for years, and Albert saw her dealing from the bottom of the deck. It was clear she had been cheating regularly. My physicist relatives believed in precise and accurate science. They refused to accept "medical science" as science and were uncompromising about this. They believed scientists needed to be proficient in mathematics and physics. They insisted "medicine" is "unscientific," or "soft science" at best, and thought medical doctors are scientifically pretentious and uninformed. In 1952 Maurice Goldhaber said to me that without question the Americans would prevail in the cold war against the Russians "because our German physicists are much smarter than their German physicists." This was partly a joke, but it also was an example of an irritating but characteristically Germanic trait: not to soften a harsh opinion no matter how annoying that opinion may be for others to hear.

CHAPTER 24:

A Posthumous Gift

Some four or five years after both Karl and Ilse were dead, I received a letter from the Kraushaar Galleries; it came on May 10th. I believe it was my sixty-fourth birthday, but I may be wrong by a year. Kraushaar Galleries were still representing the art work of Karl Schrag, and occasionally I would get a small check for sales that had been made minus the commission Kraushaar was entitled to. Recent checks had never been for more than three or four thousand dollars and they came at long and irregular intervals. I opened this letter and there was a check for over ten thousand dollars. And on my birthday too. How could Karl and Ilse have arranged for me to get a check on my birthday after they were both dead? Preposterous. But I knew that if my mother were in heaven above (a heaven in which I do not actually believe) she would have looked down and claimed credit and smiled and said, "Of course this was a planned gift for your birthday." I told myself I was being silly; I do not believe in an afterlife, even Karl and Ilse could not arrange this, and I decided to dismiss the thought that this was a gift from them.

Then I imagined my mother smiling down on me and saying, "How on earth can you get a check from the sale of Karl's work for over $10,000 on your birthday and not think it was a gift from us. Are you stupid?" Kraushaar Galleries could have looked up my birthday. It would have shown a friendly, highly personal concern for me that did not exist. They were on the whole somewhat distant in those years, as though they were planning to eliminate Karl Schrag from the stable of artists they represented. It was a time when the gallery was being run in a manner that emphasized strictly business considerations. Not long after the large check arrived, they did indeed stop representing Karl Schrag's work. When that happened, I was glad that neither Karl nor Ilse was alive to hear that Karl's work was no longer represented by Kraushaar Galleries. He would not have understood why the gallery that represented him for sixty years would stop representing his work, and he would have taken it personally. My mother would have become both angry and vicious, and she would have reprimanded Carole Pesner and Katherine Degn, and there would have been no rapprochement with the Kraushaar Galleries after that. Carole and Katherine called to ask me to meet with them. They explained to me they had decided to speak with me and Kathy separately and had already met with my sister. I commented, "I hope she took this with equanimity." From the eyebrows raised, I could only conclude this had not been the case. They explained that the gallery was moving to a smaller space, would do business over the internet, would represent fewer artists and would give fewer exhibitions, and would no longer represent Karl Schrag's work. Life went on, and some years later they decided to represent Karl's work once again. Currently they have a painting I own on consignment and my relationship with Katherine Degn is friendly.

In regard to the possibility that the check which came on May 10th was actually arranged as a gift by my dead parents,

I told myself that the test would be if it happened again on my next birthday. In the event it happened again I might well have to review my ideas and beliefs about there being no afterlife after death. The following May 10th I went to get the mail. There was no check. I was not surprised, but I was more disappointed than I thought I would be. I was also a bit relieved. My mother was highly capable, but there are limits to her influence.

CHAPTER 25:

Regarding the First Marriage, and Some Comments About the First Husband

I should comment on my mother's first marriage, which is no longer of importance for anyone except me. It certainly was important in my life as I was the only child of that marriage. After Ilse arrived in Beirut in mid-November with her mother, she and Hans Preiss married a month later. My mother once said to me, "We were young, spent a few nights together, and that was that." The marriage was troubled in that the twenty-three-year-old Ilse was beautiful and socially skilled and was well received in Beirut society, but she and Hans argued and she did not seem happy. In 1935 Ilse was ill with typhoid fever and remained ill for weeks. Hans's parents arrived from Kattowitz, and old Dr. Edouard Preiss is given credit in Hans's memoirs, written when Hans was seventy years old, for his advice and management of Ilse's illness.

Then in 1935, some months after she had recovered from her typhoid fever, Ilse learned that her father had died. Her mother wrote, saying—according to Hans's memoir, and partially corroborated by Ilse who said she felt responsible for her father's death—that in my grandmother's opinion her husband had died from concern over his youngest child being critically ill in Beirut, which had contributed to or had even caused his heart attack. Hans was angered by this, as he writes that this was "tactless, nasty, and entirely wrong." Hans thought the worsening conditions in Berlin for Jews was much more likely to have contributed to Albert's death. Meanwhile Hans was busy working in his own ten-bed clinic-hospital, delivering babies, advising patients in regard to fertility problems, and advising men who frequented brothels that they were transmitting gonorrhea (a bacterial infection transmitted by sexual intimacy/promiscuity) to their wives which often accounted for blocked-off fallopian tubes and which caused the sterility of the women. Ilse in her later life seldom discussed those times, except for saying to me occasionally, when I wrapped something up in cellophane paper in the kitchen when we were alone, that cellophane was a great invention and that even babies came into this world wrapped in cellophane. Indeed the amniotic sac in which babies live in intra-uterine life, and in which they are often still encased when they are born, is transparent and looks like cellophane. She did recall and did tell me that the collusion of pharmacists and doctors in Beirut was sleazy: the pharmacists told patients they had syphilis and referred the case to the doctor; the treatment and the medications were expensive, and the pharmacist expected the referral to be treated for syphilis irrespective of whether the rash that the patient complained of was or was not "syphilis." I do not doubt that such doings were commonplace.

In March of 1937 Ilse's sister Susie came to Beirut for a visit and stayed for a week with Hans and Ilse. She then left for Haifa and called the following week and asked Ilse to join her. Susie no doubt knew Ilse was not happy in Beirut. Although Ilse had told Hans Price she would return in a few days, Ilse did not go back to Beirut for months. Hans writes that Ilse did not return until early in July, when they reconciled. Some time later they vacationed in Switzerland, where they met Ilse's brother and his wife. Ilse's brother takes credit for suggesting they should have a baby, and in his memoirs Hans Preiss writes, "She persuaded me that she needed a child," which does not sound as though there was a great commitment on his part or subsequently any great bonding with me, his baby son and first child. I should no doubt be glad they reconciled, as otherwise my offspring and I would not be here. I was born on May 10th, 1938. Hans Preiss delivered me. My maternal grandmother arrived in Beirut shortly after I was born, and Ilse asked for a divorce so she and her little baby could leave for the USA. Europe was no longer a place for Jews.

1938 was a bad year for those who did not support the Nazis; Hitler would soon take over Austria and had plans to annex Czechoslovakia. Hitler did annex Czechoslovakia with the agreement of Great Britain and France, who preferred to appease Hitler rather than risk war in 1938, when they were relatively unarmed. Charles Lindbergh, a famous expert on aviation and airplanes since his solo flight to Paris in 1927 had made him a hero, was warning that the superiority of the German air force would overwhelm the French and English air forces. Poland would come under Hitler's control next. It was not easy to predict in September of 1938 what would happen in Lebanon. Without question, the USA would be a safer place to be in the coming years.

Ilse knew that her mother, her brother, and her sister would all soon be in New York and she no longer wanted to be in Beirut. Hans was asked to leave with them but refused. He was a successful doctor, did not think the problems of Europe would spread to the Middle East, and had worked too hard to build up his clinic to give it up. He also was classified by the Americans as Polish because he had been born in Kattowitz, and there was no chance of getting into the USA on the Polish quota in those days. My mother's brother said to me years later, "Nothing could have been more idiotic than to stay in Beirut in 1938." As a German (Jewish) national, Hans Preiss was vulnerable in Lebanon; it was only a question as to whether the French would put him in a concentration camp for being a German national (which indeed was what the French said they would do not too long afterwards, unless he joined the French Foreign Legion for two years) or whether the Germans, should they get control of Lebanon, would shoot him for being Jewish or for being a German who had avoided serving in the German army, or for both.

In 1974, when I saw Hans Preiss in Sydney, Australia, he said my grandmother had asked her son to deal with him, and that my uncle had threatened to turn Hans's sister, Franze Preiss—an eye doctor who was in hiding in Germany but whose whereabouts was known to my uncle—over to the Gestapo if Hans Preiss did not sign the papers to grant my mother both a divorce and custody of me. Evidently the father's consent was needed in Lebanon to grant a divorce and custody of an infant. This story was no doubt true, as my uncle asked to have lunch with me in 1974 after I came back from Sydney, Australia where I had visited my dying biological father. My uncle said, "It is possible I may have made some threats that were unpleasant at the time your parents were getting divorced." I explained that I had heard the story and had no problem with what was done in 1938. War was coming, there was good reason for hysteria among German Jewish refugees, and the idea that England, France, or the USA would stand up to Hitler and that they would fight and win was by no means clear in those unhappy days of 1938. The concept that the USA was an "Arsenal of Democracy" had not yet been conceived. It would have been ridiculous to say in 1938 that the USA was either an "Arsenal" or the

"Arsenal of Democracy." At that time the American military was still a very frail enterprise. The political will in the USA to get involved again in European problems was also frail to non-existent in 1938, and how to get the USA to participate in the war in Europe would be President Franklin Delano Roosevelt's main concern until the Japanese solved this problem for him with their attack on Pearl Harbor in December 1941. (That he did inspire the USA to arm, mobilize, and fight, and because his leadership enabled the Allies to win the war, is why his image on a large poster from his campaign for Governor of New York State in the 1920s hangs to the left of my desk computer. Those who quibble as to how he managed the war effort, and criticize him for not having done enough, make the mistake of looking at trees instead of at the forest—or rather the jungle, which he had to contend with.)

No doubt someone should have revisited the Hans Price problem, the divorce and its effects on me, in the 1950s or the 1960s. I could have done so, but I resisted and did not want to go there. Dealing with the loss of a parent, and reevaluating whether my loyalty was to the father who had adopted me and provided for me or whether it was necessary to seek out my biological father who had disappeared, was difficult. Now, many years later, I am still sympathetic to my mother who did not want to revisit the consequences of her divorce nor those unhappy events and times. That the cost to me of avoiding my biological father was considerable only gradually became apparent to me.

My mother said to me one day that Hans Preiss's parents killed themselves, and that too had upset her in 1937. It had not been necessary. Ilse felt that she and Hans should have tried harder to get Dr. Edouard Preiss and his wife to remain in Beirut in 1935, and again in 1937 when they met in Switzerland and/or Italy. What happened is that Hans's parents went back to Kattowitz (now Kattowice). They had their money tied up in property, and it became impossible for Jews to sell property or to convert it into negotiable form—money, bonds, whatever—and so they discovered they were poor. They then killed themselves. Ilse suggested that the sorrow over the death of three parents (his two and my mother's father) and the resentment she felt towards Hans for not doing more to help his parents were contributing factors to her divorce. I brought up Hans's parents with him in 1974 while we were at dinner together. He said his parents always managed their own affairs; they would not have accepted his advice, they wanted to go back to Kattowitz, and, once they were "land poor" (which, as they were Jews and as Jews were at that time in Germany prohibited from converting property to some negotiable form of money, was the equivalent of being cash poor), there was no alternative but to kill themselves if they did not wish to live in poverty. The son said his father, Dr. Edouard Preiss, did not want to live in poverty and "had no choice." Do I believe that my mother's comment, "We did not try hard enough to keep them from going back," is a fair comment and a valid appraisal? I do. I do so partly because Hans Price was a limited human being who did not think much about others, and empathy or putting himself in the other person's shoes was not his strong suit.

Several things are wrong with the story in regard to my paternal grandparents. The father (my paternal biological grandfather) was old and unwell, and needed help and advice. Both the son and the father, Hans and Edouard, were oblivious to the fact that the world and Poland or East Prussia in particular were changing very fast in 1937 and 1938 and the rules were now different. Edouard and Hans Preiss both thought that, as they were doctors, they therefore had a kind of immunity or protection. They believed that doctors were dignified and worthy and close to being "gods," and this status would by itself suffice to get them through hard times. Hans Preiss thought European problems would not bother him in Lebanon. That was very naive. It is true that others were naive in those days, including the very arrogant Prime Minister of England, Neville Chamberlain, who thought that he could "manage" Hitler by letting the German government annex Czechoslovakia. The agreement was signed September 29, 1938 in Munich. The hope was that Hitler would be appeased and that Chamberlain could bring or establish what he called "Peace in Our Time." In retrospect, appeasement looks as though it had been both cowardly and foolish. But there is still debate as to whether the extra time of some eleven months that was gained before war finally broke out after the invasion of Poland was or was not helpful to Great Britain. Time was needed for the British to rearm, and this time may have been more essential than trying to save Czechoslovakia and thereby prevent the Germans from controlling the considerable military and industrial resources of Czechoslovakia. It is hard to judge hard times many years after the events have transpired; those who have the advantage of hindsight like to think they know better and would have been smarter, but they may not have been smarter then and may not even be smarter now: second-guessing after the fact is easy to do, and the benefit of hindsight is used to pronounce pearls of wisdom that may not have turned out to be pearls at all, had they been effected into actual policies or deeds at the time.

But more is implicit in all this. Hans Preiss lived in a troubled world and wandered from Germany, to France, to Lebanon, to Australia, to Israel, and back to Australia; he was caught up in the French Foreign Legion and then served two years as a British military officer/doctor in 1943-44. He was very matter-of-fact; what happened, happened, and then he went on. He did not make the effort to reconnect with me, although he was in Cincinnati, Ohio in the 1950s visiting his sister. He did not want his son Michael to postpone a business sojourn in Manila because his father was dying. He was somewhat matter-of-fact about the sad fate of his parents, and quite matter-of-fact when he said that his father had no choice but to kill himself. He also was relatively unmoved when he saw the photos of my children in 1974 (ages ten, eight, and four at the time), the only grandchildren of his that existed in his lifetime. It was perhaps due to a limited imagination, but more probably it was a reluctance to let his emotions dictate his behavior as emotions were painful and were best suppressed. One goes on and suppresses regrets. Revisiting the past or revising decisions made under stress to pick up on old attachments was not Hans Price's way. My maternal grandmother was similar. Both my grandmother and Hans Preiss seemed excessively matter-of-fact about things that one might have expected to generate more thought, release more emotional turmoil or regret, or cause one to consider alternate approaches to the situation.

Hans was too arrogant and autocratic to think that his way was not "the right way." He felt that he had been smarter than others to have left Germany in 1932, and by 1938 he still thought he was smarter than others. He never wanted to leave Beirut until 1948, and he believed his first wife, my mother, once they had reconciled in 1937 and she had vowed to be his wife, should have stayed by him in Beirut. I am fairly certain that the divorce of my parents which came through in October 1938 was preceded by much hysteria, tears, anger, bitterness, and vituperation at the time. Years later Hans said she was young, emotionally labile, spoiled, the youngest child of a rich, overprotective father, and was unrealistic. She was not ready in the years from December 1933 to October 1938, when she was twenty-three to twenty-seven years old, to deal with the less-than-pristine ethics of doctors, pharmacists, patients, and people in general in the Beirut of her day. She and I arrived in New York City in early December of 1938. I was seven months old. The few times I asked my mother if people who went through hard times or experienced an unusual life, or if people who were refugees from Germany and had to start over, learned from the experience and became nicer or wiser, she said, "Not at all. People are what they are and the nice ones handle hard times honorably and the shifty ones handle hard times dishonorably. People do not change or learn to be kinder or nicer to others." My wife Jeanette says and believes the same thing. I am inclined to agree with them.

I should comment further on my mother's love of her father. My mother once said to me that in 1938 she had considered returning to Europe and Germany as she did not want to leave it as long as her father was buried there. That she might have returned to Germany in 1938, a land soon to be engulfed by warfare, because her father was buried there, was, of course, nonsense. She knew it was not a realistic possibility even when she spoke to me about it. But the emotional attachment implicit behind this idea was real enough. In 1936, when she was mourning the death of her father, a death for which she felt partially responsible, she discovered that she loved her father more than she loved her husband. Her father had met Hans Preiss only once. Before he went to Beirut, Hans Preiss had dinner with my mother and her parents in their home in Berlin. My biological father and my maternal grandfather did not particularly get along, and they never were to have the opportunity to really get to know one another. Just before dessert was to have been served, the only evening they ever were to meet was interrupted and ruined by a phone call from Cologne; Gerta, the Brunell's five-year-old daughter, was critically ill with measles meningitis. Ilse's mother had to rush off to Cologne to be with her daughter and granddaughter. Gerta did not survive this illness and her mother, Ilse's sister Susie, was never quite the same thereafter.)

CHAPTER 26:

First Jobs in the United States of America

L ife in America for many newcomers begins in Jackson Heights, Queens. In 1938 the new group were the German Jewish refugees. My grandmother, her three children, two of her children-in-law, and her four grandsons, of whom I was the youngest and the only one who had not been born in Germany, all lived near each other either at 35-35 75th Street (Oma, my mother and I lived in one apartment, and later my mother's brother and his wife and their sons, Peter and Claude, moved into that apartment and my grandmother moved into an apartment on a lower floor in the same building) or at 35-55 73rd Street, where my aunt Susie, her husband, Dr. Ernst Brunell, and Albert lived. I tagged along; my cousin Albert was four years older than me, and Claude and Peter were five and three-and-a-half years older than me, which, when one is under five years of age, is a huge difference. I only wore hand-me-down clothes until I was ten or perhaps even twelve years old.

My mother's first job was with the bookstore, French and European, that sold foreign books at Rockefeller Center. My mother was twenty-eight, good looking and blond, spoke French and German fluently, and said she was either Austrian or Viennese, which were more likely to be acceptable than being a German from Berlin in those days. She was hired after a brief interview. The first day she was at work, the management said the World's Fair was on at Flushing Meadows; the staff needed to be there in one pavilion where they had a store and that my mother was in charge of the store at Rockefeller Center, and that she should call if she needed advice. She thought it was a bit strange to leave a new young employee in charge on her first day, but she managed. My mother worked for French and European for a year (as is noted in a letter of reference that they wrote for her and which I found along with other letters after my mother died). Then she worked in some greenhouses in Queens.

But Jackson Heights was too close-knit an environment for my mother; I lived in Island Park with the Shearers from Sunday evening until Friday evening or Saturday morning, and my mother moved to an apartment of her own in Manhattan. I have her membership card in the Zionist Association of America, dated May 25, 1944, member #115818, which gives her address as 225 East 54th Street. I remember that apartment. She was then working on 57th Street and Third Avenue, a few blocks from where she lived. The florist where she worked was a large store on the southwest corner, called Goldfarb's. I remember visiting there and playing with marbles that were used for flower arrangements, while my mother did some work or finished up on some work.

A man named Rex Richards worked at Goldfarb's and later left Goldfarb's and went into business for himself. There was a florist shop called Rex Richards on the East Side for many years, and for some years there were even two. When I was in ninth grade at Friends Seminary in 1951, my mother asked me about a classmate of mine named Gail Richards and about her parents. Gail's father was Rex Richards. Gail's parents had been divorced for quite some time and her mother had remarried. My mother asked me if I kept up with the Richards girl when I was in college, and again when I was in medical school. We met Gail once on Madison Avenue by chance some time in the 1960s and I introduced Gail to my mother. There is no other classmate of mine about whom my mother inquired over so many years. Gail was never a girlfriend of mine in whom my mother might show an interest for that reason. I think Rex Richards and my mother had had a relationship, as my mother once said to me he went through a difficult divorce and needed to be taken care of at the time. Rex Richards never remarried, stayed close with his daughter Gail, and, according to Gail, over the years had many women in his life. My wife Jeanette wanted to ask my mother about my friend Gail's father after Karl had died, when Ilse might have said a bit more, but it never happened. Gail lives near me on 81st Street just east of Broadway, and we meet occasionally by chance on Broadway. Gail played a major and critically important role in my life, as in 1981 she and I went to see her friend and former classmate and roommate from Sarah Lawrence, Linda Guethe, who looked me over, thought I was so depressed that only her friend Jeanette could handle me or be interested in meeting me, and arranged that I should meet her.

CHAPTER 27:

Karl and Ilse Schrag:
the Early Years

My mother lived alone in her Manhattan apartment and dated a number of men. I met some on weekends when we would go for a walk in the park, and I recall being obnoxious in one way or another or being uncooperative on these walks in all cases. She dated Karl on and off for seven years, and I was later told he first pushed me in a baby carriage when I was one year old. Susie Schrag had introduced Ilse to Karl. After they had been married for many years, my mother claimed she owed her marriage to Karl to a careless taxi driver who drove his taxi into Karl. Karl suffered a broken wrist and had a shoulder in a sling. He and my mother would sometimes come out to Island Park on a Saturday or a Sunday and we would go to the beach, and I remember when he was in a sling. He could not dress, cook, or feed himself. He became dependent on Ilse and decided he should get married. Perhaps a general optimism in those years, as the war ended or was ending, contributed to people wanting to get married and start families.

I knew Karl and my mother were together the summers of 1943 and 1944 as I shared a room with Francis Schrag. We knew his parents and Karl and Ilse were in Gloucester, Massachusetts on Cape Ann, because Mrs. Shearer required us to write them notes once a week. I could only print while Francis could write script, so he finished his note long before I finished mine which annoyed me at the time, and this is firm in my memory. Then I learned that Ilse and Karl had gotten married on June 12, 1945. I spent July in Island Park but in August I was driven up to Portland, Maine by my uncle Hans. Karl and Ilse met me and we then took the ferry called "The Nelly G" to Great Chebeaque Island, just off Portland in Casco Bay. There one morning we discussed what my name should be: should I remain Peter Price or become Peter Schrag? This occasion deserves mention in this little attempt to write about my mother, her life, and her influence on my life, as I resolved the question that was put to me quite readily at age seven. I asked, what would my mother's name be? I was told it would be Schrag. I answered that I thought my name and my mother's name should be the same. That was accepted and I became Schrag, not immediately but when I was enrolled in the fifth grade at P.S. 6 in September of 1947.

I note here that my becoming "Schrag" had absolutely nothing to do in my mind at the time with Karl; it simply was obvious to me to remain identified with my mother and be close to her. I should add that I was not so close to my mother then. We saw each other on most weekends, but I felt closer to Mrs. Shearer who knew me better. I remember looking at some of Karl's paintings one evening and saying at bedtime to my mother that I liked some very much, they were very good, others were OK and others I did not like. I was told not to say anything critical of Karl's art work ever again. Ever since I have been unable to formulate an objective opinion about Karl's art work.

In 1945, just before Karl married Ilse, he decided to make a portrait of me and give it as a present to his new mother-in-law. I recall posing for Karl in his studio. To entertain me as I posed, Ilse sat nearby reading Hugh Lofting's *The Story of Doctor Doolittle*. Karl liked the story so much he found the second book in the series, *The Voyages of Doctor Doolittle*, and gave it to me. The portrait of me was in my grandmother's apartment for many years. After she died in 1970 it was returned to my parents, and I found it stored in the cellar of their house in 1997. I had it reframed and it now hangs in my dining room. The portrait is a drawing with me in a red short-sleeved sweater, colored a reddish pink in the drawing. I remember that sweater; it was one my mother had knit for me, and my cousin Fran had an identical one which his mother had knit for him.

My mother wanted to appear refined and did not want to appear hungry when Karl would take her out for dinner prior to their marriage. So she always had a sandwich before they went out so she would have no difficulty concentrating on the conversation rather than on the food. My mother continued to make an effort to eat slowly and leisurely, and equated that with refinement and good manners. But late in her life, when she was tired after having served half a dozen guests a delicious meal that she had prepared herself, as she always did when they had company, she would forget herself and eat several desserts in a short time. It was how she rewarded herself after a successful dinner party.

These notes are mainly about Ilse. Writing about Karl would require me to write about his art work, and I am not prepared to be Karl's art critic as I could not do his work justice. He wanted to be loved and thought of as a great artist. I loved Karl and he was always kind to me and interested in me. I have memories of him from 1944, when he was thirty-two years old, until his death in December 1995, when he was eighty-three. I learned from Karl to be high-minded about others, not to pay attention to gossip, to value knowing who you are whether others do or do not appreciate you, and that becoming a philistine is not a solution. Karl also taught me to appreciate what was unusual and different even if I did not understand it or like it (or them) right away. His friends included many highly original and unusual people, and many had peculiarities, but he and Ilse taught me that these made them more rather than less interesting. He taught me to enjoy walking over rocks on stony beaches, and to appreciate nature, and to enjoy skipping flat stones over the water by the seashore, something he was good at; seven or eight hops per stone thrown was not unusual for him to achieve. One day, after he returned from a visit to the doctor, Ilse asked what the doctor had said to him about his abdominal pains; he replied, "The doctor said I am not a truck driver," to which his wife responded, "I could have told you that."

He was always devoted to my mother, who was usually right but could be abrasive. When I did finally go to meet Hans Preiss/Price, Karl was not offended and was gracious. The only concession I made was when he asked me, some years after I first met them, whether I kept up with my Australian half-brothers; I said, "No, I did not." This pleased him and cost me little, and may even have been true at that time. (Only in recent years do I see one of my half-brothers more often. He and his wife come from Sydney to New York City regularly to visit their son and his family, which includes two little grandsons, their only grandchildren, at their son's home in Brooklyn.)

Karl and Ilse both taught me to be high-minded and to appreciate the best in imperfect people. Maurice Goldhaber was an unscrupulous money raiser. He was also one of the world's great scientists. There was an intrinsic contradiction, a mixture of benefit and discomfort whenever one was involved with him, a mixture of being made complicit in intelligent and original projects accompanied by unusual and onerous demands. It was a privilege to associate with him even if he involved you in his fundraising, which brought with it new opportunities and insights as well as trouble. I believed that Gertrude and he were not just nosy scientists who bombarded you with questions and interfered in your career and who might steal your ideas, but rather that there was always some benefit from being involved with them.

Leonard Baskin was an artist and collector who antagonized people and did not pay his bills promptly. He was a misanthropic, asocial, introverted person with a macabre view of the human condition that he depicted in his art and especially in his renderings of birds. But he was a talented and highly original artist.

Dr. Charles Ragan was a fine doctor and a great teacher and a Catholic Socialist. He knew how to drive aggressive, mercenary, right-wing Jewish doctors insane with rage with his emphasis on "sharing," and he was not an anti-Semite.

Fred Farr did wonderful jewelry, sculpture, pottery, and paintings; he was also a heavy drinker and womanizer and handled his first wife's depression and mental breakdown poorly.

Andre Racz was a gifted artist, although he behaved badly to his wife in Chile, whom he divorced and with whom he had many children, to whom he also behaved badly (as we were told by a mutual friend, his divorce lawyer).

Ben-Zion was an interesting artist who painted and did sculpture. He felt safer going to a pediatrician than to a doctor who treated adults, and claimed he had found a pediatrician who had agreed to care for him. He also went into a tirade if one cut bread; according to him bread had to be torn rather than cut.

Karl's oldest friend, Lucien Goldschmidt, was not only a pedantic, finicky bookworm and superficial intellectual who was more interested in books' bindings than in their content; he was also a great connoisseur of prints and books, introduced Henry Mattisse's series of prints called "Jazz" into the USA, and was a cultural resource.

Karl's friend Bill Hayter had moved from New York City back to Paris, France; he was an Englishman who had been raised in England, was married and later divorced from his wife Helen Philips (an American woman raised in California, I believe, who did sculpture), and, during the early 1950s, when McCarthyism was frightening anyone with leftist ties, said things that were unquestionably anti-American. Karl would quote his friend Bill Hayter as having said in the early 1950s, when we were discussing Senator Joseph McCarthy one evening at dinner in our kitchen, "America is the worst place; in America even the Jews are stupid." Then Karl would laugh. Ilse, however, did not laugh and did not like such a comment. Karl and Ilse often said they were not police or tax collectors and whether or not gifted artist friends of theirs paid their taxes was not their responsibility; Karl would then add that, of course, he would not be friends with murderers. Karl and Ilse did not expect their friends to be perfect, nor were they.

No one ever mentioned Ilse's first marriage; Ilse's life with Karl was the most important thing in her life. I think that the failure of her first marriage was viewed as a disgrace and as something not to discuss. Ilse did not want to fail a second time and devoted herself to Karl's needs, his friends, cooking and entertaining, maintaining a busy social life, spending summers in Maine where he liked to work, and bringing up both me and Karl's only child, Kathy, who was born in 1947. I remember going to court with Karl and Ilse at about that time, seeing a judge in his courtroom, and being told that Karl had now adopted me. I was told that I should be pleased and gave it little further thought at the time.

Some years ago I came across a passage in a book by Marguerite Yourcenar called *Souvenirs Pieux*. M. Yourcenar, the author of *Hadrian's Memoirs* and other novels, was the first woman writer to be elected to the Académie Française. In her book *Souvenirs Pieux* she describes her family, Belgian Catholics, around the time of the First World War. She explains that the relations between relatives were highly structured and notes the importance of and the emphasis on the relative status of one relation to another. What happened in the Yourcenar family sounds very similar to what happened in my mother's family: M. Yourcenar states that in her family mistakes such as a bad marriage or a scandal or an affair were simply forgotten or denied ever to have existed or happened. The more modern approach to divorce, which nowadays may include that the divorced couple meet recurrently at such mutual family events as funerals or weddings—and that their new respective marital partners greet one another with handshakes, or hugs, or even kisses—was unheard of in my mother's family over half a century ago and was probably unheard of in Youcenar's family as well. The world in the 1940s was quite different: there were no jet planes and no worldwide travel, and the refugee community in the 1940s and 1950s looked to the future and shunned the past.

After May of 1945 there was a surge of optimism and happiness that the war was over and that life was getting better. Ilse and Karl were not wealthy, but they were comfortable enough so Ilse could stop working, stay at home, and care for a child if she and Karl were to have one. On their return to New York after the summer on Great Chebeaque Island, Karl and Ilse lived together in his studio apartment at 15 West 67th Street. There was one bedroom and a large studio. I visited on weekends. They often had company on Saturday nights, so I went to sleep in their bedroom and was later carried or was walked with assistance in my sleep into the studio. I slept next to Karl's printing press, which had long spokes that were handles to turn the wheel of the press. These spokes were detachable by being unscrewed and when I was there they were placed on the floor so I would not hit them at night when I woke up or sat up. There was a standing lamp with a glass lamp shade that I upset one morning; the glass shade shattered. Ilse became hysterically angry at me. The problem was that it was a Sunday morning and the shade could not be replaced immediately in those days on a Sunday, and Otto, Karl's eldest brother, and his son Peter were coming for lunch. Ilse was eager to impress them with her housekeeping and homemaking skills and I had allegedly ruined it as I had broken that elegant lamp. That was one of the first major emotional thunderstorms my mother exhibited to me.

In the 1980s Jeanette asked Ilse if I had lived with her and Karl immediately after she and Karl married. Ilse said I had, which was not the case at all. I corrected her by saying I only came to live with them in 1947. My mother told Jeanette that was not so. I do not believe she had forgotten. She did not want to admit that she and Karl lived in Karl's studio apartment together for two years before I came to live with them. Ilse felt guilty about this when she spoke to Jeanette. I remember all those details well, as Karl and Ilse moved into the brownstone on 95th Street in June of 1947, and I never lived with them or went to school in Manhattan until I started fifth grade at P.S. 6 in September of 1947. I had been apprehensive about leaving my school in Island Park, where I had gone for first through fourth grades, for a new school. I also was worried about living with Karl and Ilse. I had been living in Island Park with the Shearers for four years and was not sure I wanted to leave them.

Kathy was born in December of that year. I remember when she was born and remember thinking that my getting many gifts from Karl and Ilse for the new baby's birthday was a pleasant surprise. I should add that I never thought I was unwanted, nor did I feel rejected in any way because Karl and Ilse lived on 67th Street without me. I saw them on weekends and knew that Karl had been a bachelor, had lived alone, and needed time to adjust to new responsibilities and his new life. He and my mother came to visit me several times in Island Park before they were married, and on those visits Mrs. Shearer and my mother were very solicitous and considerate of Karl. On or just before those visits, I was told to be on good behavior both by my mother and by Mrs. Shearer. I knew then Karl needed some encouragement and appreciation when he came to visit. I recall being encouraged to always be very appreciative of any gift that he gave me. I liked Karl but I was never in a hurry to move in with Karl and Ilse.

In 1946 I never thought that my mother should have asked me to live with her and Karl. Even after I was living with them and we were a reconstituted "normal" family with mother, father, son, and baby daughter, I would occasionally go out to Island Park to spend a weekend there with the Shearers. That my mother might feel guilty and not want to admit I had not lived with her and Karl right after they married in 1945 was a sentiment that developed or existed only much later.

There were other times when my mother was upset and in great emotional distress, although I do not think she was emotionally unstable as she never totally lost control of herself. However, if others did not agree and thought she was unstable, I can understand why they might think so. The times my mother got inappropriately upset are vivid in my memory. When Daniel was born in January 1966, I insisted on picking him and his mother up from the hospital and said my mother and Karl were not welcome that morning; they were only welcome that afternoon as mother and newborn needed to settle in at home. This caused anger and tears as Ilse felt excluded or cut off or relegated to uselessness by the arrival of the new baby. However, when Karl and Ilse showed up at our apartment in the early afternoon that same day, all was forgotten and everyone was friendly, happy and smiling as though nothing had ever happened. Perhaps Daniel, then a brand new baby, made a contribution by being sweet and utterly dependent on his elders. His mother and I, the proud father, could fulfill his needs. It was a happy time and a good day that had started badly for no good reason.

Then there was the time when I tried to make conversation with Sally Avery, the widow of the painter Milton Avery, and was not doing very well. Sally Avery was quite an old lady by then and I had trouble finding a subject to talk about with her. It was important to my parents to impress this woman and my mother was angry thinking I was not making enough of an effort. Another outburst came at a time of great stress; Paul had been dying from cancer for some months and now was coming to the end of his life. I went over to see Karl and Ilse at their house just to say hello and keep them company while we had a drink together, or perhaps it was coffee. Suddenly my mother, who had been apparently normal although not cheerful as was only appropriate, attacked my shoes. She asked how I could come to her house wearing such shoes that were in total disrepair. I looked down on my shoes; they deserved a shine but were not worn out. Clearly my shoes could not possibly be the real problem. This was an unpleasant, bizarre, and inappropriate outburst, but we were all unhappy; she could not comfort Karl easily which always upset her. But after a while she quieted down.

Her outbursts, when directed at me, were of little consequence as I never kept grudges against my mother whose emotional lability under certain circumstances was not really that disturbing to me. But others with whom she was close were not so happy nor so forgiving when she reprimanded them.

CHAPTER 28:

Some Schrags and Sulzbergers

Karl Schrag came from what my mother's family called a fine family. His maternal grandfather, a man named Ferdinand Sulzberger, had been a very rich man. In the decade 1900-1910, Sulzberger and Sons was one of the five major meatpackers in Kansas City; the others were Cudahy, Swift, Wilson, and Armour. In 1916 the business was sold to Wilson, as the German name "Sulzberger" could not compete for contracts for meat for the U.S. Army. Ferdinand had eight children by three wives. Karl's mother Bella was born and raised in New York. On a trip to Germany, before the First World War, she met Hugo Schrag, a young lawyer, married him, and lived in Karlsruhe through the First World War. Hugo and Bella retired to Zurich, Switzerland in 1931. After Hugo died in 1939, Bella came to New York City to join her sons, Paul and Karl. As Bella was a native-born United States citizen, neither she nor any of her sons had any difficulty to move to the United States. Bella developed a pituitary adenoma, which was fatal in those days, and died in New York in the early 1940s. Her doctor was

Dr. Milton Rosenbluth, a professor at NYU. and a friend of Bella's brother Dr. Marion Sulzberger, who was the chief of dermatology at NYU. Dr. Rosenbluth was for many years Karl's doctor as well.

Bella's other brother, Nathan Sulzberger, an interesting man, lived in a large apartment on Central Park South. I was in Ellsworth, Maine, staying with Paul and Susie Schrag and my cousins, their sons, in 1952 and could not sleep one night after Paul told us that Nathan, whom I knew and had visited often with Karl, had been operated on that afternoon and they had amputated his left leg. Nathan never married, had many friends, was a chemist by training, believed in and owned many shares of the Schering Plough Corporation, and invented and made money from his patent on "Aspergum," i.e. aspirin in a chewing-gum form.

When Nathan died, Karl said I should attend the funeral. Karl said I knew him and had visited him numerous times, and Uncle Nathan had even attended my bar mitzvah luncheon at our home. Karl thought going to a funeral where the person was not that close to you was the best way to learn what it was like to attend a funeral. I was a little tense but agreed to go. I was sitting at the funeral next to my mother listening to some elderly female friend of Nathan's speak in a somewhat theatrical way as she eulogized her friend Nathan Sulzberger. Then I looked at my mother; she was shaking so much that the bench we were sitting on was shaking. I was surprised and imagined she was overcome with grief and therefore was sobbing with her entire body. But my mother accepted life as it came and she had not been so close to Karl's uncle, so it was puzzling to see her so upset. Then I saw her face was covered and she was trying to suppress her laughter. I then had to keep myself from laughing. Ever since then, whenever I attend a funeral, which always makes me tense, I think of this time when Ilse started to laugh and I remind myself to not be too tense and also not to laugh as a way to relieve the tension.

Paul was the lawyer for his uncle's estate and Uncle Nathan had more feeling for family than one had expected; his beneficiaries were his extended family. Some of the shares of Schering Plough stock that my parents received from Uncle Nathan were later given to me. I received them in a custodial capacity for my children, and these shares sent them through college. My uncle Paul, Nathan's nephew, told us he spent much time cleaning out Nathan's apartment and wondered what to do with his uncle's ashes. It was a sunny day; Nathan had loved his apartment high above Central Park South with a spectacular view of Central Park to the North, and Paul took a large spoon and distributed Nathan's ashes to the wind high above Central Park South one spoonful at a time. Nathan Sulzberger died sixty-five years ago.

From left to right: Susie (age 15), Hans (age 13), Ilse (age 9), and Else Szamatolski, taken in Berlin in 1919.

From left to right: Hans, Else, Susie, Albert, and Ilse on a walk. Taken in Berlin in 1923.

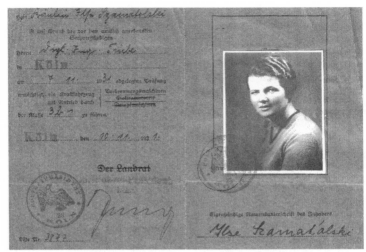

Exit visa for Ilse Szamatolski to travel from Berlin to Beirut in 1933.

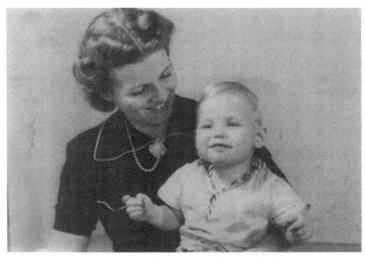

My mother and me in Jackson Heights in 1939.

From left to right: Peter Samton, Claude Samton, my mother, me, and Albert Brunell in Far Rockaway, 1943.

Kathy, my mother and me, sitting in our garden at 127 East 95th Street in 1954.

My mother and me in the far corner of our garden wearing our favorite jackets, 1955.

A photo of my mother probably taken in the early 1960s.

My sister and me, 1953.

Left to right: me, my son Jonathan, my mother, and my son Daniel in front of our house in Maine, 1979.

Karl and Ilse Schrag, 1995.

Karl, my mother, and me in 1945.

CHAPTER 29:

Getting Professional Help from Lawyers and Doctors

Karl said his mother, Bella Sulzberger Schrag, was respon-sible for referring Dr. Rudolph Baer (1910-1997) to her brother, Dr. Marion Sulzberger (1895-1983), who later was Baer's mentor. The story is no doubt true as it originated with Karl, whose statements in regard to these matters were always reliable. Dr. Baer studied in Basel, Switzerland, and grew up in Strasbourg in the Rhineland not far from Karlsruhe were Hugo and Bella Schrag lived. I recall that Dr. Baer lived on the east side of Park Avenue in a large building between 93rd and 92nd Streets, not far from my parents' home on 95th Street. Occasionally Karl met Dr. Baer on Park Avenue.

Towards the end of his life, Karl had a small skin cancer behind his left ear. He went to NYU to see Dr. Baer. Dr. Baer removed it. When they went to pay the bill the receptionist said that would cost $800. (This was in 1992 or 1993.) My mother said, "Has Dr. Baer become senile? This is Karl Schrag, whose mother Bella Sulzberger Schrag introduced and referred Dr. Baer to her brother, Dr. Marion Sulzberger. Dr. Baer owes his whole career at NYU in the last half century and his being the successor to Dr. Sulzberger, Karl's uncle, as chairman of the dermatology department here for twenty years, to Karl's mother. You had better discuss this fee with Dr. Baer." This was more than the receptionist had been trained or authorized to deal with. She consulted Dr. Baer, returned with a smile, said she had told Dr. Baer what my mother had said and there would be no charge.

My uncle, Paul Schrag, Karl's brother, handled my parents' legal problems—wills, taxes, and real estate matters like buying their brownstone or the place in Maine. He was always gentlemanly and considerate, but his reassuring attitude that signified there were no serious problems did not satisfy my mother. The appearance of a patronizing attitude derived from the fact that Paul knew that Karl had no legal problems; therefore, Paul was inclined to think none of my mother's legal concerns or questions were serious. However, my mother thought her legal concerns were too readily dismissed. She was also annoyed that both Paul and her brother received restitution from Germany after the war for the suffering they had incurred, while she had not received any compensation. She thought that she and I had suffered as much as they had suffered. But Paul explained that as we had no established positions from which we had been dismissed, neither Ilse nor I, unlike Paul and her brother who had been dismissed from legal jobs, had any legal claim. We might have had problems, but there was nothing anyone could do about them and they certainly would not merit financial compensation. Paul explained she had voluntarily left Europe at age twenty-two in 1933 and, therefore, had no legal claim. I was born in Lebanon in 1938 and I too had no legal claim.

Actually there was and is an inconsistency under restitution laws. My mother and I had no claim for financial compensation under existing laws, as neither of us had been dismissed from an important position, but we had been made stateless by a law that deprived German citizens who were living outside of Germany for political reasons of their German citizenship. In 1951, when that was subsequently acknowledged as having been illegal, she and I could reclaim citizenship not only for ourselves but also for all our descendants until the end of time or until the end of Germany, whichever would come first. I will return to this later, but here I'll simply point out that claiming there was no case for restitution is inconsistent with acknowledging that there was a valid claim for restitution of German citizenship. Somewhere one should acknowledge or admit that unquestionably being rendered "stateless" caused inconvenience, anxiety, suffering, and hardship; compensation might indeed be justifiable and appropriate.

Ilse believed the laws were inadequate for the calamities that had occurred, and that the lawyers were sanctimonious and unwilling to admit the laws regarding restitution were inadequate to compensate for what had happened to people. I think she was correct. My cousin Albert used to say, when he felt someone was giving him a "brush off"—and this was often the case as he worked as a lawyer and bank inspector for the U.S. Treasury Department—"What are you running here? Is this a Swiss insurance company that will not pay out on a life insurance claim without a death certificate, and therefore if one had died in a German concentration camp would not pay out on the life insurance because the fact that the Germans gassed and cremated people without issuing a death certificate is deemed by the Swiss insurance company the family's but not the insurance company's problem?" Sometimes the rules are foolish and inappropriate in view of the actual circumstances.

CHAPTER 30:

Reaction to My Resurrection
of Dr. Henry Price

My mother was not happy when she heard I had found Hans Price in the Medical Directory of Australia (where there was only one Henry Price, M.D., University of Berlin 1928), had written to him, and had a ticket to go to Sydney to meet him. Ilse suggested I should keep in mind that Hans Price was never interested in me, never did anything for me, and was only interested in his career. My mother's sister told me to give him her regards; she said he and she did not like each other, but added that I would find him to be very intelligent. I told both my mother and her sister that I had consulted a psychoanalyst who suggested I go, and that I was not going for pleasure but was acting in accordance with medical instructions. I should note here that in 1970 Kathy Schrag Wangh suggested I consult her father-in-law, Dr. Martin Wangh, a prominent psychoanalyst. He quickly zeroed in on my having been adopted by Karl and referred me to a colleague for psychotherapy and to search for my biological father. Meeting my biological father was of more importance for my mental health than anyone in my family, including myself, had realized.

Discovering that you need to attend to an important problem that you have previously avoided is unpleasant. I had never been to Australia and therefore had never been able to meet Hans Preiss. But once I admitted I would have met Hans Preiss had he lived in New Jersey, the only obstacles to meeting with him were that I would have to buy a plane ticket to Sydney and take a twenty-two hour flight across the Pacific ocean from New York to Sydney. Australia was easier to get to in 1974 than it had been in 1944. I had written Hans Preiss a letter and he responded with an invitation to come to meet him, and I then went to Sydney.

After I returned from Sydney in 1974, my mother was less than pleased with the book of memoirs that was written (from notes Hans Price left) by a writer whom Hans's sons in Australia had hired to work their father's notes into a book. My mother referred to the book as "nothing but lies," but the book was interesting to me. One day her brother-in-law Paul mentioned to my mother he had just read this book, a book that I had lent to him but which my mother would have preferred he had never seen. She became somewhat defensive and then a bit belligerent and said something to the effect that her grandchildren were far superior to his and that one could not even compare their relative accomplishments. I was not there and can only surmise how upset and unpleasant she had been. But clearly what had upset her was the guilt she had carried all those years and the related "shame" of her divorce in 1938. She wanted to say that despite the disgrace of divorce and a foolish marriage to "an awful person," her grandchildren were wonderful. No doubt she did not do this tactfully. No doubt she was upset. No doubt I had made matters worse for her by lending that book to Paul. But he was a lawyer and had some interest in seeing if anything truly libelous was included in the book, and had asked to see it for allegedly legal reasons. He also was a professional who should have realized that my mother's underlying anger had nothing to do with the relative accomplishments of his versus her grandchildren. Ilse was not at her best, but I thought Paul should have understood that she was dealing with what had been for years treated as a "shameful" or foolish past. She was merely asserting, in her way, that the shame and stigma of her bad marriage did not compromise or diminish the worth of her grandchildren. Paul, as a lawyer, should not have let himself be so personally affronted—but I say that while admitting I was not present to hear the exact words.

Paul never really forgave my mother. When he was dying some years later, in 1992, he told Karl that Karl was welcome but my mother was not. Paul also excluded others, including his close friend Dori Furth, a lawyer with whom he had collaborated for years. My mother did not hold grudges; she always expected to be forgiven for whatever she said when she was upset. Paul was her bother-in-law, and she had been a friend of Paul and Susie's for fifty years. Karl thought that as Paul was not well and under treatment for his cancer, one should respect his wishes. I got involved as I thought my mother was hurt. It was a stressful time for all, as Paul would not be cured. I told Karl that when he went to visit Paul the next time he should just come with his wife; if Ilse was not welcome, then he too should not come in and say that he could not stay if his wife was not welcome. Karl took my advice and did take Ilse on his next weekly visit to his brother. "Were you both let in?" I asked. They were, and from then on Ilse occasionally accompanied Karl to visit Paul and there never was any perceived offense. I am not surprised; Paul was the most elegant and refined person I knew and was helpful to others in many ways, and he dealt with his own last illness with grace and courage.

CHAPTER 31:

My Relatives:
Are They My Patients, or Am I
Just Working for My Mother?
(Or Perhaps Both.)

Thanks in part to my uncle's difficulty in acting both as a professional and as close family at the same time (two different roles that may conflict and cannot always be reconciled), I have thought a great deal about how to care for or resist caring for or giving advice to relatives. I tried to develop criteria for caring for relatives. My preference in all cases is not to care for them, out of respect for the patient's/ client's right to get angry with his doctor as well as to protect myself from having a family member resent me permanently in case I "screwed up badly" or in case they had a problem neither they nor I could deal with. However, I am a good doctor and cannot always avoid getting involved. Being cared for by family does have the advantage that the provider knows you better than some impersonal stranger, but that too is a double-edged sword that may work to the patient's advantage but may also do the opposite.

My mother's sister Susie was a case I did not want to take on; she was a doctor's widow and even more difficult and opinionated than my mother, and I refused to take her on as a patient when she approached me one day at a family gathering. She complained about me to my mother. My mother, to her credit, told her older sister she could afford to find a doctor. Getting rid of Susie was not that easy. She and I were close and I had lived with her for several weeks starting in June of 1980 when I suddenly needed a place to live. My living with her sister annoyed my mother, but I reassured her it was temporary and that I would move into my own apartment in Manhattan in a few weeks. "What is a young man like you doing living with that old lady?" was my mother's initial comment. But it was then that I knew—and I knew before anyone else—that Susie was becoming demented and would not be able to live alone for much longer. Albert and I spoke about this and he felt that he and I should manage his mother together for the time being.

Some years later, in the mid 1980s, Susie showed up in my office. She said she needed me to remove the big toenail on her right foot. I said I no longer did that, but she insisted I should do it. She said there were only two doctors she would go to—me and Dr. Rosenheim, an orthopedist in Queens whom she knew. "But did you not tell me that Dr. Rosenheim is dead?" I asked. "Yes, he is dead," she replied. Susie was a widow, living alone, and her memory was now impaired. I knew her well, and knew if I did not help her she would simply neglect herself. After I had removed the big toenail, she complimented me on having done it very well. She said she had done this procedure often for her husband in his office (Ernst Brunell was severely nearsighted which made it hard for him to do minor surgery), and could not have done it better herself. (Susie acted for her husband in the following roles: office secretary, surgical nurse and assistant, social worker for follow-up care, consulting psychologist, office cleaning staff, chauffeur for emergency house calls or hospital calls, ambulance driver, bookkeeper, file clerk, and clinical consultant.)

I also told Susie some months later she should take some medication I would prescribe for her to stop her recurrent atrial tachycardias. She replied she would not take any form of digitalis. I told her I had something new, or rather new to her, and reprimanded her for practicing medicine based on her knowledge derived from her husband Ernst who had died in 1967. She accepted this criticism and started to take Inderal, not all that new a medication by then, and reported to me some weeks later that I knew something she did not know, as her paroxysmal tachycardias no longer occurred. My mother appreciated that I looked after her sister and was impressed that Susie felt much better on the Inderal. But Susie was getting more confused and her memory was progressively worse. She and Ilse saw a neurologist whom I referred to them, but he could only confirm progressive early dementia. From then on Ilse saw Susie every week. She was often included for supper at my parents' home, and once or twice also came with Karl and Ilse to my house. Although Ilse had been for many years eager to keep her sister's life separate from her own, this changed once she realized her sister was no longer well.

One day Jeanette, Jeanette's son Benjamin, my son Jonathan, Susie, Ilse and I were sitting at the circular dining table in my parents' large kitchen. Karl had not yet joined us. Susie was trying to get the various relationships straight. She said to Jon, whom she had not seen in quite a while, "That is your mother?" and pointed to Jeanette. We corrected her. Then she turned to Benjamin and said, "That is your father," pointing to me. We corrected her again. Then she said "Peter and Jeanette are married but you are not Jeanette's son," pointing to Jonathan. Then she repeated all the relationships but again got one wrong. We started to laugh. I thought Ilse would get angry, as she might think we were being impolite or were making fun of her sister. But as Susie wrestled with these various connections we all suddenly realized we were getting confused ourselves and we all started to laugh. My mother then said, "It all does not really matter."

My aunt Susie lived alone in Jackson Heights and could more or less still manage with some assistance. But one day her son Albert called me to say she had fallen. I diagnosed a broken hip from what Albert had described, and she was hospitalized at Lenox Hill Hospital. This was sometime between 1985 and 1988 when I was there. After her hip surgery, she never really got strong enough to walk well or to leave the nursing home where she was placed, and she died some months later. My mother said she thought Susie might have lived longer had the staff at the nursing home in New Jersey not been impatient with this difficult woman, who needed by then to be fed. According to my mother, they had fed her too quickly as the staff was in a hurry, she had aspirated, and then had gotten an infection in her lungs and died. I shrugged my shoulders and said I did not know if my mother was right or not. In fact I think she probably was right, but it was my cousin Albert's business to decide if the nursing home in New Jersey had been reputable and/or abusive. My cousin Albert and I were close and he asked me to speak at his mother's memorial service. I said some things but was speaking before a critical audience, and Ilse was not congratulatory about my remarks. Her comment was, "You make a lousy rabbi." I cannot remember whether I winced or laughed. At least Albert was pleased with my talk.

I was a bit turned off by my family after I returned from Australia in 1974. I had lots of problems both at work and in my personal life, and I was still seeing Dr. Baudry. My uncle and his wife had a major anniversary one June. (I believe it was their sixtieth wedding anniversary). Dr. Baudry suggested I not go if I felt disaffected or estranged. The story with Hans Preiss was such that I had reason not to be admiring or adulatory of my uncle. But I told Dr. Baudry that it was easier to go than to give offense. If I went, it would take only a little bit of time; I could be there, be friendly, and leave. After two hours it would be over. If I stayed away, I would be reprimanded by my mother for months and hear about the inappropriateness of slighting my uncle and have more pressure to show up there for Thanksgiving, so my attitude was "Let's just get this over with and forget it." And that is what happened. The reason to go was that my mother would not like me to offend her brother. She herself was allowed to do so, and did so on occasion, but I should not. I perhaps sound like a wimp, but I found it easier and less consuming of my time and energy to be superficially involved rather than give offense. I had balked at complying with a request from my aunt Margot, my uncle's wife, to call some cousins of hers in Sydney while I was there in 1974. I had enough problems of my own to contend with in Sydney and my aunt's request was not a high priority. She was a very correct person and my failure to have called these people disappointed and annoyed her. I said to her, somewhat to her surprise, "The world has gotten smaller. Just call them yourself from here; Sydney is not that far away by phone nowadays."

There were family members whose illnesses I had to pay attention to. Paul once called me, saying it was an emergency. He had acute vertigo, could not lift his head without getting dizzy and nauseated, and was in bed. I gave him some medication, reassured him that he was not having a stroke, told him he would be better in forty-eight hours, and told him that in the meantime he should just lie still in bed. He had hoped I would have some more effective, sophisticated, and more rapidly curative treatment but, when he was soon back to normal, was appreciative enough. The other family members I got involved with were usually referred to me by my mother. She would say, "Albert is having surgery for his back, will you call him?" Or she would say that her brother is worried, because his daughter, my cousin Annette, "has a thyroid problem." I would then call, and in Annette's case arranged for her to be cared for by a surgeon at Columbia. My mother would expect me to reassure her brother, who was a great worrier when members of his family were ill.

When Henry was in his eighties, he decided he needed hip surgery as he did not like to be seen walking with a cane. My mother was worried he might not survive this operation and told him he would be better off just using a cane for a few years. My contribution was to tell Ilse she was wrong and too involved, and to stop practicing medicine. Then Annette called to ask me if she and her brothers should encourage their father to have his surgery done in White Plains Hospital, which would be far more convenient for their mother, Margot, who could get to White Plains easily from Scarsdale, or should they take their father to Manhattan and the Hospital for Special Surgery? I recommended having the surgery done in White Plains and that worked out just fine. All this was done with some surveillance by my mother, who would have criticized me if things had gone badly. But Ilse was also generous with praise when she was pleased. Late in her life, my aunt Margot Samton had polymyalgia rheumatica, and this was controlled with cortisone-type medication. Unfortunately, the cortisone washes out the calcium from bones and Margot had some vertebral fractures due to collapsed vertebrae. She was miserable, and Henry, who tended to worry, was miserable. Henry and Margot always went to Scarsdale or White Plains doctors and managed their affairs without consulting me, which was fine by me and which in fact I greatly preferred. When things were going badly Henry called my mother to say he was worried. Then my mother would insist that I get involved.

I was lucky in that the timing of my involvement with Margot's collapsed vertebrae worked to my advantage; I called my uncle and asked how many weeks his wife had been complaining. He recounted numerous visits to doctors and neurologists and several injections, some of which had been painful but none of which made Margot happier, and said this had now been about ten weeks of misery. I said that in my experience little can be done for collapsed vertebrae, the pain lasts quite some time, but by twelve weeks she should be feeling better. My uncle thanked me, and two weeks later he called to say that my aunt was much better and that I had been right. My mother heard from her brother that I had been helpful, but Ilse only mentioned to me that Margot was better; she would not thank me. It was just expected and assumed that I would be helpful, and in most of the cases referred to me by my mother, I was.

One year I arrived in Deer Isle, Maine for what was to be a one-week vacation. I was hardly in the house when Karl and Ilse said their close friends David and Sally Lund needed me to make a house call on them; Sally had terrible back pains. I went to see Sally only because my mother insisted I go. Sally wanted me to come up with a quick cure which, unfortunately, was impossible. She said she had hoped I could help her as I had allegedly helped David with some back pains (of which I had no recollection whatsoever). She was in so much pain in the week following my visit that she agreed to have more diagnostic studies. She turned out to have a serious problem, and died a year or so later from a malignant tumor in her spine.

I have no doubt that my mother's fragile emotional health—or, rather, her previous emotional breakdown—was a consideration when her family recommended she divorce Dr. Preiss when Ilse was unhappy in Beirut in 1935-1938. The decision to get her out of the marriage and out of Beirut was encouraged by her mother and siblings, who knew or thought Ilse was fragile and that Beirut was or would be unsafe. Her family was concerned for her and thought that she might not be able to face the complications of being in Beirut during the war. (What happened later is that Hans Price's second wife and their two children lived in Beirut without him while he was in the French Foreign Legion and again later when he was in the British Army. I can only wonder and speculate as to whether my mother would have endured or survived in that predicament.) My mother's siblings considered Ilse permanently fragile, which was not quite the case; she was "emotionally fragile" and prone to emotional outbursts, but some of these outbursts were on purpose and could be generated as needed to serve her interests. Nonetheless, both Henry Samton and Susie Brunell did consider Ilse as someone not to be taken too seriously because she was emotionally fragile and unpredictable. I occasionally thought they also did not take me seriously when I was little, and that may have been true too.

CHAPTER 32:

My Mother and Her Daughter as Viewed by Me From a Considerable Distance

My sister and her husband Larry wanted to help my mother and Karl get up to Maine, and offered to drive them from Boston to Deer Isle. The drive had become a little bit too much for Ilse and Karl by the early 1990s. Unfortunately Larry and Kathy's car broke down several times on the drive up to Deer Isle. It was a hot day and Karl was miserable. Nothing upset my mother as much as Karl being miserable; it was her purpose in life to protect him. I gather Larry got an earful of abuse for not having a car that functioned. Again, I was not there and can only imagine the scene, but it must have been unpleasant. I think my brother-in-law would admit that after this episode he never was quite as enthusiastic about his mother-in-law, nor quite as appreciative of being in her company as he had been previously. That Ilse was awful and abusive when upset is true; that she did not hold grudges is also true. But both Paul and Larry never entirely forgave her as they both had been recipients of Ilse's wrath. I too at times had been the recipient of her wrath, but my mother was my mother and I loved her unconditionally. She understood me far too well and we were too close for me to ever take offense for long. The rest of the world was less forgiving. I understood and sympathized with Larry. In Paul's case, I thought he should have understood that Ilse's emotional outburst was motivated primarily by a desire to say her grandchildren were not afflicted with any character defects inherited from their paternal biological grandfather.

Did my mother offend her daughter Kathy in some way so that Kathy held a grudge or some resentment? As I left for college at seventeen, when Kathy was seven, there were many years when Kathy and Ilse interacted without my knowing any details as to how they interacted. I had no inkling of there being any friction. But either there was cause for resentment or—in retrospect, and after some years of psychoanalysis at the Anna Freud Institute in London when Kathy and Larry lived there—Kathy was left with the belief that she could have or should have been treated better. I suspect that my sister and brother-in-law had some financial constraints and were not in agreement with the way Karl and Ilse managed their money. But Karl never let anyone other than Paul give him financial advice, and my mother left financial decisions to Karl. Over the years, in my opinion, Karl and Ilse were actually quite careful to be fair and distribute financial help equitably to both their children; that is my personal opinion and I am not interested in discussing it with anyone else.

I know little about my sister's relationship with Karl and Ilse in her childhood, except I know that the summer of 1952 was problematic. I stayed with family; Kathy stayed in Island Park with Mrs. Shearer, was unhappy there, and vomited up her orange juice every morning (and received it every morning nonetheless, she told me). Karl and Ilse were

traveling through Italy at the time. Ilse recalled staying in a
five-star hotel in Taormina, Sicily, and being unable to eat a
thing, as she had indulged in unripe figs that she had picked
off the trees and eaten, and afterwards was sick for a few
days. I remember that summer well, as I had appendicitis
and an appendectomy and wrote to my parents about it. In
recent years, after Ilse's death, I have never discussed these
matters with my sister. I do not want to hear that there were
problems, and I do not believe I would hear that there were
no problems. I knew some years ago Kathy felt close to Karl
and loved and admired and even adored him, while in regard
to her mother my impression is simply and best summarized
by the phrase "less so." Ilse had good will but could not help
being offensive at times.

I also thought that Kathy and her children were not particularly considerate of my mother the last years of her life.
Sometimes they ridiculed my mother among themselves,
and I remember being offended when I heard them. Kathy
refused to stay overnight in the same house with Ilse after
February of 1996 and Ilse never understood why. But clearly
Kathy did not want to be burdened with any caretaker role
at that stage, even for just a weekend. She had stayed in the
house with our mother for some weeks in December 1995
after Karl died, and perhaps she had decided after that very
difficult time "never again" would she stay overnight in the
same house with her mother. Karl had adored Kathy and
never criticized her; he would leave it to his wife to do or
say whatever was deemed necessary, and they had a "good
cop–bad cop" system to deal with their daughter that probably contributed to Kathy's great fondness for Karl but some
wariness of her mother. That Kathy revered her father and
was more reserved in regard to her mother is something that
I was reminded of whenever I went to Deer Isle. There are
photos of Karl, in particular a poster showing Karl at his

press, and a large portrait made by his close friend Joseph Breitenbach (a professional photographer who photographed a number of his socialist and leftist friends, such as Wassily Kandinsky and Bertolt Brecht, when they were all living in Paris in the 1930s) prominently displayed in the house or in the barn. There is not one picture of my mother, although she and Karl, in the thirty-five summers that they spent in Deer Isle, Maine, were involved in what was very much a joint venture.

My views on these matters can also be challenged as being far from objective and based on scanty or incomplete information. But I think it is correct to say that Kathy and I had different experiences and points of view of our parents. Ilse was a different mother to her daughter than she had been to me, her son. She and Karl were supportive and friendly to all the young men Kathy brought home, and were very solicitous of Kathy's in-laws. I never heard any objection to Kathy's getting married relatively young. They had more difficulty accepting that I got married at age twenty-four. They were correct but not solicitous toward my in-laws during my first marriage.

CHAPTER 33:

My Mother Tries to Immunize Me to Female Charms

When I was between the ages of seventeen and twenty-three, I was not home much. But on occasion I was present when friends of my parents came for afternoon tea or dinner. If they had daughters or nieces, they would bring them along on the theory that there was a nice young man in the home and "one never knows." This was a great mistake, as no involvement between me and any girl whose family brought her to my parents home ever resulted, even though many of these young ladies were quite lively and attractive. But the occasion was co-opted by my mother to teach me about women. When they had left, my mother and Karl would discuss their recent company as well as the young ladies, whether they were pretty, whether they seemed interesting, what they had talked about, etc. Then they would ask me if I had liked them or thought any of them attractive. I would make some mild and fairly noncommittal comment. Then my mother would zero in on a particular feature; she would suggest that I probably liked those big blue eyes one particular girl flashed every now and then, or say I probably was taken in by the blond long hair that she swished back with a toss now and then, or she would say I probably was taken in by her nice figure, or even go so far as to say I probably fell for the way she pushed forward and slightly lifted her chest to call attention to her breasts. Invariably my mother would say, "You probably fell for that nonsense." What was uncanny was that my mother almost always cited the very feature of the young woman that I had indeed either noticed or found particularly charming. These sessions served a purpose quite unlike anything the parents of these young women might suspect was going on or would want to have happened; they were exercises my mother devised in an attempt to make me less susceptible to superficial charms. Did these toughening-up exercises accomplish anything? I hesitate to claim they immunized me to anyone's potential charms to a significant degree, but perhaps they did. My mother definitely thought her comments about these young women was a very necessary part of my education.

CHAPTER 34:

Karl and Ilse's Social Life in Deer Isle

Karl and Ilse were friends of Dori Furth, who like my mother was a German Jewish refugee whose family had lived in Berlin. Dori had been Paul's legal secretary; he had urged her to attend law school, which she did by going to NYU at night, and in 1950 had been admitted to the New York Bar. She was visiting us that summer in Harborside, Maine, and was worried whether she would find a job. She actually found a job soon after at Strasser, Spiegelberg, Fried, and Franck, a law firm founded by German Jews and today known as Fried, Frank, Harris, Shriver, and Jacobson. For fifty years she was in their wills and estates department, and one said of Dori that she could put together a complicated will at three in the morning after being awakened suddenly and have it finished in ten minutes. She came to Maine regularly, spending a week with us and a week with Paul and Susie. My mother did not object to professional women but, when they complained about their life, always said, "Don't be sorry for them. They want the best of both worlds and that cannot be."

One summer evening in Deer Isle, Dori, who like many lawyers liked her scotch before dinner, was sitting on the porch chatting with Karl. Ilse was getting supper ready. After supper my mother said to Karl that she was tired of him and Dori enjoying their drinks and chatting while she cooked. From then on Dori had to stay at Goose Cove Lodge when she came to Deer Isle. But I have memories of having had many good times with Dori. She and I often went on bike rides, and she had a wicked underhand side-arm throw and could hurl a soccer ball with a whiplike motion further than either Karl or I could when I was fourteen years old. Her side-arm throw, to me, was reminiscent of Ewell ("The Whip") Blackwell's, a great pitcher for the Cincinnati Reds baseball team in those days (the early 1950s) who had a powerful side-arm underhanded throw. In those days I followed baseball closely. Dori called our game of throwing a soccer ball "schleuderball." "Schleuder" is the German word for hurling, catapulting, slinging, or flinging.

One summer the group of friends who summered in Deer Isle and socialized together decided to go to the University of Maine in Orono to see an art exhibit at the museum there. Orono is half an hour's drive beyond Bangor, so from Deer Isle it would be a two-hour drive and possibly a bit more. The group of friends were mainly artists from New York, but not exclusively. The majority of my parents' friends in Deer Isle fit two out of three criteria: they were Jewish, from New York, or were artists (or in the art world). David and Sally Lund, Leon and Meta Goldin, Karl and Ilse Schrag, and Carole Pesner fit all three criteria. Leonard and Lisa Baskin fit two, in that they lived in Northhampton, MA. Shirley Kaufman and her husband were from New Orleans, Louisiana and were art collectors and fit two. Bernard and

Joan Weinstein were not in the art world but did buy paintings, and they lived in greater New York and fit two criteria.
Stephen and Pam Pace fit two criteria in that they were artists
and lived in New York City. And then there was Pat Burke,
who was neither Jewish nor from New York but was an artist
with many girl friends, some of whom were Jewish and/or
from New York. On arriving at the museum that Saturday
morning, they discovered the museum was closed on weekends in the summer time. They decided this was a problem
for my mother to handle. She got hold of the security people
and explained that this group of important artists had come
from Deer Isle never expecting that such an important show
at such an important museum would be closed at the height
of the summer season on a summer weekend, and would it be
possible to allow this distinguished group to see the show?
Some phone calls were made, the museum was opened up for
them, and the Deer Isle group did get to see the show that
day. Ilse was good at persuading people to do her bidding.

In Deer Isle there is a picnic bench and table under some
cedar trees a short distance from the house, with a view of
nearby birch trees and the meadow that extends for a dozen
acres or more into the distance. It is a nice place to have lunch
on a beautiful, sunny summer day. The problem is that wasps
hover over the table. My mother loved to have lunch at this
table and believed she could control the wasps by making
them an offering. She would place a jar of jam at the far end
of the long picnic table and reassure everyone present that
the wasps would concentrate at the readily available jar of jam
that she had set out for them. But wasps are a bit like people;
there always seems to be an original thinker or one that does
not understand the game plan. Many wasps prefer someone
else's lunch rather than their allotted jam. Usually one could
brush away one or two wasps that hovered over one's sandwich, but sometimes a swarm of wasps, perhaps not liking the

flavor of the jam in the jar my mother had provided for them, would succeed in undermining the courage of the attendees at the lunch, and all the people in attendance except my mother would quickly retreat into the house behind screened doors and windows. My mother would be disappointed, and as we gathered together the lunch to move it into the house, she would often say that we, her children and grandchildren, were all just cowards and were too easily intimidated by a few wasps.

CHAPTER 35:

Some Interactions with Her Granddaughter, My Daughter Deborah Schrag

When my daughter Deborah was going to the Ethical Culture School on Central Park West and 65th Street, my mother would occasionally pick her up from school. Ilse bought Deborah some new ice skates and they would go from Deb's school to the Wollman ice skating rink, which is in Central Park and fairly close to the school. They would take a taxi home after skating for an hour and we would join them for supper at my parents' house. One day they arrived at 127 East 95th Street and discovered that Deb had left the relatively new skates in the taxi. Ilse was angry. But Deb said she had been trained to always remember the cab driver's license number, which is always posted and visible to passengers in the back seat. Ilse was very impressed; she called the taxi company, they located the driver, and the following day he returned Deb's skates to her.

When my children were little I asked my parents what they wanted to be called by their grandchildren. When my oldest was born, my parents were in their fifties. They were not ready to be called a grandparent-type name and said my children should call them Karli and Ilsie. So my children were on a first-name basis with their grandparents long before I was. But after hearing my children call their grandparents by diminutives of their first names, I decided that it was silly for them to be able to use their first names but that it was not acceptable for me; I started to call them Karli and Ilsie on occasion, or rather I referred to them by those names and avoided calling them by any name when I addressed them in person.

In the late 1980s, Deborah spent a year in Israel learning Hebrew, living for a while in the Negev on a kibbutz, and then working in Tel Aviv. My mother worried about Deb's safety; she said it made her anxious to have Deb so far away, among Bedouins (desert dwellers in Arabic), and on several occasions asked me how she was and expressed concern. I said I would give her Deb's phone number in Tel Aviv; she was by then staying in Dina's apartment, along with Dina's son Yochai who was then not yet Deb's husband (or perhaps he already was, I no longer am certain). If Ilse called there, either Dina, Yochai, or Deb would be on the phone. I posted the phone number for Dina's place in Tel Aviv and suggested the times that were best for calling. Over the next few months my mother would invariably ask me when I visited whether I had any news from Tel Aviv or from Deb. I would say "no," whereupon she would smile and say she had a long conversation that morning or the previous day with Dina (more often than with Yochai or Deb), and would give me a summary of how things looked over there as far as Dina was concerned. And she stopped worrying about my daughter's safety. Ilse liked to be able to make contact and liked being able to get news without being dependent on me for information. I encouraged her to call whenever she wished, saying, "It's not that expensive to call Tel Aviv and you can afford it." So she called often. I almost never called as I would miss Deb more if we spoke on the phone and I knew she was O.K. My mother liked to keep up with news from Israel and reminded me that she and her mother had been there in 1935 and had ridden around the walls of Jerusalem on donkeys.

CHAPTER 36:

Hot Dogs, Apple Pie, and Chevrolet May Be All-American, but Cadillac is Definitely French

As a little boy I, of course, knew German quite well, as my mother spoke German perfectly and my family spoke more in German than in English until 1943. My mother's English in those days (the early 1940s) left a bit to be desired; I recall correcting her when I was four by saying, "One says 'feet,' not 'foots.'" Ilse would tell us that she passed the exam for getting a driver's license, but when they had asked her, "What does 'cattle crossing' mean?" she had answered that she had no idea. She had elaborated by saying she knew the word "tea kettle" but had not heard of "cattle crossing." The examiner passed her nonetheless, dismissing this answer as a faulty response due to language barriers. That my Germanic relatives could not pronounce English words correctly and that they made mistakes in grammar was an embarrassment to me when I was little.

In the summer of 1944, when I was six, my grandmother had rented a house for her children and grandchildren in

Long Beach, Long Island. My mother had a first cousin once removed, Anne-Marie Abeles, the daughter of her cousin Else and Mohr Abeles, who came for a visit in a large maroon-colored Cadillac convertible which my cousins and I admired. My mother pronounced the word "Cadillac" in the French way, which I found strange and peculiar. I corrected her and explained it was pronounced "Cad-ill- lack" in English. However, she ignored me and continued to pronounce the word her way. Many years later—and by then I had studied French for some time and could pronounce most French words correctly (more or less)—I was on top of Cadillac Mountain on Mount Desert Island in Maine. A plaque on the top of the mountain referred to Antoine Laumet de la Mothe, sieur du Cadillac (1658-1730), an explorer of the Great Lakes region and of the Maine coast (now known as Acadia National Park), a scoundrel, a trader in furs and alcohol with the Indians, and an administrator who founded the village of Fort Pontchartrain du Détroit which later was where the city Detroit ("le detroit"—the strait) sprouted up. Leland and Murphy used the name of the founder of Detroit, the city in the USA where their cars were built, as the name of their luxury car which first appeared in 1902. My mother was dead by the time I stood on Cadillac Mountain and read that citation and said, "Damn, he was a Frenchman and she was right after all."

When I was a boy I objected to being told that things I considered to be "American," such as "Cadillac," were in fact European words or names. My mother sometimes would remind me that there were many European or French words in English. When she was learning English she readily expanded her vocabulary by latching on to words that were valid English words and were identical to the same French word in meaning and spelling. She would favor such "English" words, as it was easier to use words with which she was already familiar. "Buffet" was a word she used often. But how to pronounce it correctly in English was not so obvious. Her grandchildren sometimes corrected her pronunciation. She would then urge them to pronounce it "correctly," with the correct French intonation for the "u"; this was something which they never really could do to their grandmother's satisfaction, despite having had several years of French in high school. Insofar as I could determine, the different generations never could quite agree as to how to pronounce " buffet."

When we were in Maine in 1946, I was eight years old. Ilse and I read *Grimm's Fairy Tales* together, or rather I had to read them to her. I was not yet all that proficient at reading in English, but reading, whether in English or German, was something I was encouraged to do and we read together every day after lunch. I remember the edition of *Grimm's Fairy Tales* was in Gothic Script, and this at first bothered me and I complained that it was hard to read. But my mother did not accept my objection to Gothic Script, and she was correct; I soon had no difficulty reading it. I am still sentimental about some of those stories but am not sure whether it is because I like the stories or because I remember those times.

CHAPTER 37:

Privacy: "What? I cannot check up on my own children and grandchildren?"

One of the concepts that my mother was oblivious to was the idea that children or grandchildren should have privacy. That the older generation needed to respect the wishes and privacy of the younger was just not part of the Germanic culture. Related to this was an attitude that there were many things—and especially anything unpleasant, such as death—about which children really had no need to know. I, for example, had liked Rita's mother. Rita was a cousin of my mother's whose elderly mother was friendly, lively, and appeared regularly at family gatherings. Then Rita's mother was never seen or mentioned again; I was ten years old and was not deemed worthy of being told she had died. I was not so close to this woman that I needed to be protected, yet was close enough that I was annoyed that I had not been informed that she had died.

I was occasionally given a lovely book as a gift. Then it would disappear; my parents had decided they wanted to read it or that I was too young to appreciate it. Karl in particular found wonderful books that appealed to him, which he would give me as gifts only to take them for himself to read a week after I had received the "gift." That was annoying, but kids and their needs did not always count for that much. A box of tools I had been given was lost by movers; I was never told; it just disappeared. The same thing happened to a fishing pole which was lent or given to one of my cousins, although it had been given to me as a present. Once when Ilse came back from a visit to her daughter and grandchildren she seemed less than happy. "What happened?" I asked. She told me she had napped in her granddaughter's bedroom and then had looked through some drawers and papers and noticed some homework that had been returned. She looked at it and then discussed some math problems she had seen in the homework. Her granddaughter and daughter were offended that my mother had invaded her granddaughter's privacy. Ilse was hurt; she had not intended any offense nor did she really understand why there had been a fuss over what was, from her point of view, simply grandmotherly interest.

CHAPTER 38:

Interaction with Her Granddaughter Marina Wangh: "The Lady Dost Protest Too Much, Methinks"

Marina once told her grandmother that her teacher had asked her to describe her grandparents and their background. Marina had said that her mother's parents were German Jewish refugees who had grown up in Germany. Marina said the teacher then said, "Oh, your grandparents are holocaust survivors?" and Marina said she had answered "yes." Ilse was annoyed and ridiculed the teacher for promoting a total misconception. She told her granddaughter it was silly to go to school to learn things that were just plain wrong. Ilse explained she had left Europe in 1933, had arrived in New York in 1938 before the Second World War even had begun, and had never been held up in a concentration camp as a foreign national. So "holocaust survivor" was a misnomer. Unfortunately, this is a case where Shakespeare's line needs to be cited: "The lady dost protest too much, methinks" (*Hamlet*, Act III, scene II). Ilse's denial was technically correct and would hold up under cross examination in a court of law; she had avoided Germany and Europe after 1933 in that she never was there during wartime (Second World War) and had arrived in New York in December of 1938. But this is an example of the many levels of "truth" that need to be looked at to approach the reality of what happened. The "facts" by themselves may obscure rather than elucidate events, as the choice of the words "holocaust survivor" that were used was misleading. Ilse was actually indulging in apophasis: denying something forcefully because it was actually true. Although she was technically correct in claiming she was not a "holocaust survivor," she was unconsciously disingenuous as her life story was very much affected by the events in Germany between 1933 and 1945. More importantly, her eagerness to disassociate herself from people who were badly traumatized by the second world war had other unintentional consequences; it predisposed her to think everything in her life was OK. She had a right to be optimistic and not feel sorry for herself, and even may have been right to be proud of having escaped from Berlin in 1933. But the traumas of life in Beirut, an unpleasant separation from her husband in 1937, a temporary reconciliation, the death of her father in 1935 shortly after he was dismissed from his job, a painful divorce in 1938 some five months after having a baby, and a need to rebuild her life were not trivial problems that could be swept away by saying "the problems of Europe were not my problems and did not affect me."

Worse, from my point of view, was that certain interests of mine were lost or obscured or hidden by this valiant effort to affirm that she was not affected by the war in Europe, when the opposite was closer to the "truth." The term "holocaust survivor" was technically incorrect when applied to my mother; it was indeed too narrow and too specific to apply to her case. But by asserting she was not a "holocaust survivor" my mother was indulging in self-deception, and was trying to avoid confronting problems in her past. Since I never saw my natural father until 1974 and as we never dwelled on the events in Beirut in detail, her disregard for her past cost me more than it cost her. To assert that I was not affected by the Second World War was still more ridiculous than to assert that she was not affected by the Second World War; it was I who had lost a father yet was still attached to him, and who wondered about his exploits in the French Foreign Legion and/or the British Army, and who persisted (from age four through age eight or nine) in hoping he might come back despite the assertions and assurances of others that he would not. It is not that my mother never alluded to her problems with Hans Price. She said she did not like Beirut and her life there, and found nothing was reliable nor as it should be. She also once said there was a nurse who killed herself and that she probably had believed Hans Price would marry her, but I never was able to go back to those days or that story in detail with my mother.

My mother did not disassociate herself from refugee causes. She and her friend Susie Schrag worked for "Self Help," the refugee agency that did social work and aided people with finding homes, jobs, friends, relatives, lost money, etc. But my mother did not really believe in Holocaust museums, and when the Stephen Spielberg movie *Schindler's List* came out with good reviews and attracted large audiences, my mother said when she heard we were going to see it, "Why on earth do you want to see that depiction of concentration camps and other garbage?" Nor was my mother an admirer of the writer Elie Wiesel, who won a Nobel Prize for Peace in 1986 and whom my mother dismissed with the derisive epithet that he was "a professional Holocaust man," meaning that one should not make a profession out of writing about other people's misery. She also meant that one needs to be

positive about life and people and not be fixated on crematoriums and concentration camps.

In recent years there was an article in the *New York Times*
about men who had served in Viet Nam, had been lonely,
and had found solace, sex, and affection with women in Viet
Nam. Many fathered a child with their Viet Nam partner,
and later abandoned both the woman and the child. Several
such men were mentioned as now having gone to Viet Nam
to seek their child. Several such men had found their children
and were overjoyed. An interval of thirty-seven years was
mentioned. Evidently men in wartime under stress father and
later abandon both the child and the mother. It is not a new
phenomenon. But something else struck me: one of the men
who found his now grown up child had been happily married
for some decades to an American woman who knew nothing
of the previous liaison or of the child the man had fathered.
The reappearance of the newly found child stressed the wife
and the resulting acrimony led her to ask for a divorce. This
was precisely one of the considerations that had inhibited me
from seeking out Hans Price; Karl and Ilse had been very
kind and good to me and I did not want to stress them and/
or complicate their lives with my personal problem. This
sounds in retrospect very self-effacing, but actually it was
not. It is not self-effacing to refuse to see someone whom
one might simply fight with or want to hit. I would need
more insight into myself, into the psychology of arrogant,
priggish, self-righteous, moralistic, and self-centered profes-
sionals, and into the effect "hard times" can have on people,
before I would be ready to confront Hans Preiss.

CHAPTER 39:

German Jewish Refugees Resurface in Manhattan's Washington Heights, "The Fourth Reich"

When I think of where I was in 1972, I realize that the chances of my avoiding my past were rapidly becoming virtually nil. I was at that time an internist at the Columbia Presbyterian Medical Center, with an office in the large doctor's office building on West 165th and Fort Washington Avenue. The neighborhood at that time was inhabited by a large German Jewish refugee community. Many were my patients and many reminded me of people I had known. When these people became ill they got anxious and previous anxieties often resurfaced. It was hard to ignore their past. I had dozens of such patients. Many had been forced to do terrible things to stay alive in concentration camps; some spoke about these things after they knew me quite well, while others refused to say anything about those times, and others only very reluctantly spoke about their past. I realized I had more understanding for them than did other people. I did not want to play at being their psychiatrist, but empathizing with them somewhat enabled me to handle them more easily. I realized many of them had not gotten as much help or sympathy as they deserved.

My colleagues at Columbia played some dirty tricks as the politics at the medical center became complicated and contentious. I began to surmise what my natural father may have felt, may have had to put up with, and how he might have behaved under the stress of life as a medical doctor in Breslau among the Nazis, and again later in Beirut where the doctors were abusive to patients and each other. I recall a discussion I had with a senior professor of medicine at Columbia who had been my nemesis. He was Jewish, had gone to Harvard, and was the son of a Jewish obstetrician/gynecologist. I went to him to explain to him that I knew, as did he, that the "malpractice" accusation that he had made against me was false and was simply an old trick: to antagonize a patient deliberately and then accuse the doctor of "malpractice," because the patient who had been rendered extremely angry had become uncooperative and unmanageable, and then accuse the doctor who could not control or manage the uncooperative patient appropriately of being incompetent. I remember our discussion and my telling him of my natural father who had practiced among the Nazis and was familiar with such tricks. This professor commented, "Your father must have been a real bastard." I remarked, "That is a fair and interesting question. Who was more asinine and/or hysterical for no really good reason: you and your colleagues who behaved like total jerks in 1973 because they objected to paying a tax and wanted more money and because the world was not going their way, or my father in 1938, when the world was heading in a direction that was unfavorable to German-Jewish doctors? At least one can say for him he had something to get excited about: living as a political refugee in the Middle East, Hitler running Germany, Neville Chamberlain trying to appease Hitler by giving him Czechoslovakia, Jews being rounded up and hounded out of the professions in Germany, and an air battle for Britain looming on the Horizon." On hearing I came from a family of German Jews this professor had said, "I can see how someone from your background would find it difficult to practice here." I was forced to rethink and reformulate some of my ideas about practicing medicine at Columbia; I thought I was dealing with colleagues who were gangsters, but they thought I and the vice chairman for medical affairs of Columbia, who was at that moment one of two people under consideration to be the president of Columbia University, were gangsters.

CHAPTER 40:

127 East 95th Street, and Our Neighbors There

Karl and Ilse moved into the brownstone on East 95th Street in June of 1947. That was a difficult summer for Karl and Ilse. She had to stay on bed-rest and was expecting a baby in December. I think Ilse had a "partial placenta previa," an obstetrical complication due to a low-lying placenta. I cannot remember exactly why or how I know this, but I do believe this is correct; it is possible that my mother and I discussed it years later when I was studying obstetrics. She was reasonably knowledgeable about this, as she had been the wife of an obstetrician and even, on occasion, his assistant during deliveries in Beirut. It is also possible that I deduced this on my own, in that I had heard Karl and Ilse discuss, after Kathy's birth, their relief and their concerns and worries during the pregnancy. Although I did not know the term "placenta previa" at the time Karl and Ilse discussed their concerns, I may have deduced or concluded that that had been the problem after I was a medical doctor. I was sent away that summer of 1947; I spent the summer traveling in New York state with my cousin Albert and his mother, my aunt Susie. We traveled to Lake Placid and to Niagara Falls in the Brunell's new dark blue 1947 Pontiac, which featured a windshield wiper on the rear window. Albert and I were very much into identifying cars and the features of the different models at the time. I remember when Kathy was born that December; my mother's brother-in-law, Dr. Ernst Brunell, delivered Kathy at the Wickersham Hospital in Manhattan. Ernst's specialty in Cologne had been obstetrics. A nurse was in our house for a week or two once the baby and mother came home. Ilse disliked this woman who did not want her to be up and about, and she was only too glad when this woman was no longer needed. My mother regarded her and treated her as a nuisance.

For the next fifty years Karl and Ilse lived at 127 East 95th Street. The top floor was an apartment in its own right. The first tenant was Captain Albert Zanger, the former captain of the Normandy, an ocean liner of the French Line that had been sabotaged in New York harbor. He appreciated that Karl and Ilse spoke French. A few months after he had moved in, he was joined by his new and much younger wife whose first name was Andrée and who had red hair. They lived there for two or three years, and sent my mother two pheasants every year at Christmas time. But these two large pheasants arrived with all their feathers and neither Karl nor Ilse wanted to pluck the feathers. So the pheasants got thrown out after a few days, and to this day I have never tasted pheasant.

The Zangers moved to Forest Hills and stayed in contact with my parents. When we went to Paris in 1958 Captain Zanger had become and was then the President of the French Line. We stopped by at his very elegant, large office in Paris that summer and said hello. Uniformed guards took us into his office. He spoke with us for a while, then said he was busy and could not join us for a drink, but called his wife who met us for a drink on the Champs-Élysées. Karl was surprised that she would come to meet us and have a drink with us all by herself in a public café, but she did. Ilse and she liked each other. I should add that access to the top floor in my parents' brownstone was only by using two flights of stairs that required you to pass by all the rooms in my parents' home; the doors of these rooms could be closed but there were no locks on any door except the bathroom.

One of the great features of my parents' house on 95th Street was the garden. Along the walls on each side were vines of morning glory that climbed up strings we attached to the nearby wall. There were chrysanthemums that bloomed every fall, and irises, both blue and purple, that bloomed in the spring and summer. In the left far corner was a rose bush on which small yellow roses bloomed every May. For a few weeks every spring the garden was brightened by many tulips of a variety of colors. In the summers, zinnias and marigolds in yellow and orange were in the middle one of the three flower beds. To our surprise, ten-foot-tall sunflowers came up one year and then for many years thereafter. These had not been planted, but came from seeds that we had provided for birds who scattered them in the garden. My mother loved this garden and periodically refurbished it with new bulbs or planted some flowering plants that were available from local greenhouses. Occasionally the neighbor's son forgot his keys, came into our house and, with a little boost from my mother, climbed the garden wall between our house and his so he could enter his back door, which was usually unlocked.

I cannot summarize all the connections my parents made with the people who lived on 95th Street over the next half-century. The street was by no means an elegant one in 1947. Half the brownstones were rooming houses for multiple occupants and half were private homes. If the rooming houses predominated over the private homes the value of real estate would go down; if private homes predominated, property values would increase. It was by no means clear in which direction the block would move. In early 1948, Al Hirschfeld and his wife Dolly Haas moved into the house across the street and a bit closer to Park Avenue. The Hirschfelds and my parents were for many years the residents who had lived on 95th Street the longest. The Hirschfeld's daughter Nina was the same age as my sister Kathy and was her playmate and friend. Dolly had had a career as an actress in Germany and was exactly as old as my mother. She came from Mannheim. Dolly and my mother met often in the street and spoke in German together. I remember Dolly in an Alfred Hitchcock movie called *I Confess*. She was a good actress but Al did not want her to continue her career.

The Hirschfelds always gave a gala New Year's Eve party. Karl and Ilse were often invited but never went. They preferred to spend the evening with their own friends. I recall that when I was in high school I heard that Richard Burton and his wife Elizabeth Taylor would be at the Hirschfelds' and I encouraged my folks to go but they did not. I was always an admirer of Elizabeth Taylor. At that time I considered her to be the most beautiful woman in the world, but that was only if one excluded the young Ingrid Bergman, Ava Gardner, Gene Tierney, and Jean Simmons. I had heard Elizabeth Taylor would wear an enormous new diamond necklace and I would have loved to have been there; or, if I weren't able to go, my mother's appraisal of Liz would have interested me. While my mother and Dolly met often and were, if not close friends, longtime neighbors, friends, and acquaintances, none of us ever spoke to Al Hirschfeld, who secluded himself unless you were in the "theater world." After he died in 2003, just before he would have turned one hundred, someone called me saying that they knew I had lived on that street and had known many of the people who lived there, and could I give them anecdotes or stories about Al Hirschfeld. I laughed and said I was sorry to have to disappoint them; I had known Nina and Dolly over several decades (but not well) and had spoken with them often, but I never exchanged a word with Al in my entire life. The person who spoke with Al Hirschfeld was my sister Kathy. She had been at Nina's house when she and Nina were children.

Kathy in the late 1990s found a portrait of Nina that Karl had done when Nina was a young girl. Nina, like her mother Dolly, had flaming red hair which made both Dolly and Nina quite striking and even more so when they were seen together. So one day after Dolly had died and after we had rummaged through old paintings of Karl's after he and Ilse had died, Kathy went to visit Al and was led by his new wife upstairs to Al Hirschfeld's studio on the top floor of his house. Kathy showed the painting to Al; he was over ninety but immediately recognized it as a portrait of Nina, and accepted it appreciatively as a gift. By then Al had been living in his house on 95th Street for over fifty years. I should add that both Kathy and I went to see a movie called *The Line King* which was about Al Hirschfeld and his family. It included scenes of 95th Street, where neither of us lived any more. Neither of us had seen Nina in decades and Dolly was dead, but our parents had lived across the street from the Hirschfeld's for over fifty years. My favorite anecdote from this movie is told by Al Hirschfeld, when he was asked if he was ever threatened with a libel suit for one of his cartoons. He answered that the libel laws are not easy to apply to cartoons and then told the following: He was not a friend of the playwright David Mamet, whom he portrayed in a cartoon that was not too flattering of Mamet's features. To his surprise, Mr. Mamet wrote asking for permission, or offering to buy the rights, to put this cartoon on the

Christmas/New Year's card that Mamet wanted to send to all his friends.

The brownstone a few houses west of my parents' house belonged to Maria Riva, the daughter of Marlene Dietrich. Marlene often visited her daughter or came to her home, and we knew this as Marlene would walk her daughter's dog in the street. If we saw her and Karl was at home, we would say to Karl, "Marlene is walking her daughter's dog, go out and see her in the street." Karl was an admirer of hers and Karl could do a very good rendition of the song "Lili Marlene" in German.

A few houses to the right of my parents' house, between them and Maria Riva's house, lived Rabbi and Mrs. Langer. He was the Rabbi of the Synagogue on Lexington Avenue between 95th and 94th Streets. They were Alsacians, so my mother and they spoke in both German or French. He was fifteen years older than my mother and had fought for Germany in the first world war and, as the Germans did not trust the Alsacians to fight against the French, had been sent to the Russian front. There, according to his daughter Janine, he was saved from the front line when a Jewish quartermaster saw him and another Jewish soldier praying and putting on the teffilin. The quartermaster recruited them as his assistants, probably saving them as the quartermaster corps was a far safer place to be than being in the trenches. (This anecdote is included to show how no stereotype is really valid; who would imagine that two Jewish soldiers in the German Army in 1916 were saved by a German Jewish army officer who recruited them for the quartermaster corps and favored them because they were observant Jews?) My mother took me to the garden of the Langers several Septembers or Octobers, as they had a Succa and she wanted me to see it and know what it was. Their daughter Janine is now (as of 2016) eighty-five years old, and until recently I often met her either on Broadway or at my neighbors' whom she knows as they attend the same synagogue. She and I still share memories of 95th Street in the 1950s.

Janine in the 1950s distinguished herself by catching the neighbors' ten-year-old year old son throwing a rock at the Langers' dinning room window while they were having lunch on Saturday after going to morning services. She started to hit him; he was scared and said she had better stop, he was the grandson of John Foster Dulles, the U.S. Secretary of State. The story I heard at the time from my mother was that Janine said, "What, you are the grandson of Dulles? Then you deserve a few more," and smacked him a few more times. Forty or more years later I discussed this episode with Janine when we both were at my neighbors' house for supper one evening celebrating the feast of Succoth. Janine assured me that was not what she had said. She had said, "If you are Dulles's grandson, then I am Eisenhower's niece." She then slapped him. The boy was the son of Lillias Dulles Hinshaw, a Presbyterian minister and Dulles' daughter. (Dulles had three children; one son was a history professor in Austin, Texas, and the other son was a theologian who became a Cardinal in the Catholic Church. The family was strongly anti-Communist, deeply religious with clergymen in the family for generations, and Dulles, as Secretary of State, spoke disparagingly of Communism as "Godless terrorism.") Reverend Hinshaw lived across the street from my parents and the Langers, but a bit closer to Lexington Avenue. She came to see the Langers the day after Janine had apprehended her son, apologized for her son's behavior, reassured the Langers he would be punished, and peace between neighbors and local clergy of different denominations returned to 95th Street.

Also on that side of the street lived Alfred Drake. He sang in the lead role of *Kiss Me Kate*, a musical adapted from Shakespeare's *The Taming of the Shrew*. This ran on Broadway for years. They had two daughters about my sister's age, Candy and Sandy. Karl thought that the Drakes were anti-Semitic. He referred to them as the "Drecks" (dreck means "dirt" in German). Exactly why Karl felt this way is not known to me. I never had any personal contact with them some sixty years ago. One of the Drakes' granddaughters, I believe Candy's daughter, is now married to my son Daniel's old school friend, Jon Grossman. Jon Grossman and his wife live in Newton, and he is a lawyer in Boston and has reconnected with my son Daniel, his friend from childhood, who lives in nearby Cambridge.

The photographer Joseph Breitenbach was a close friend of my parents and came for dinner often. He was Bavarian, and in southern Germany "Josephs" are often called Seppi after the Italian Joseppi. Sep or Seppi was someone I had known for years. One day Ilse said I could no longer call him Seppi; he was now an elderly and highly respected photographer and I should call him Mr. Breitenbach. I objected. I said I had been calling him Seppi for so long he could not possibly object unless I was introducing him to an audience of strangers. My mother accepted this. Bernard Malamud presented a similar problem, and told my cousin he no longer liked being called "Bernie"; he was now to be called "Bernard." My cousin Eddie Schrag reached out and, holding Malamud firmly by the right shoulder, said, "Bernie, we have always called you Bernie and you will remain Bernie to us." My mother was standing next to her nephew and just smiled. She and I thought Malamud was getting pompous and handling his renown poorly. But to Malamud's credit, he looked at my cousin Eddie and said, "O.K."

CHAPTER 41:

Arch Supports as the Key to Health and Happiness

My mother and Susie Schrag were great believers in taking care of one's feet. My mother often mentioned that her father would come home in the evening from work, take off his shoes, change his socks, put on other shoes, and only then relax. I scoffed at such nonsense when I was younger but, for the last two decades, I do the same most evenings. When Fran and I were boys we were fitted for "arch supports" on several occasions. At various times I had to insert arch supports into my shoes every day. Sometimes the added arch support was made of leather, sometimes it was metal; once it was leather covering a metal base. If we went to buy shoes the preference was for shoes with good "arch supports." I think it must have been a Germanic concept that high arches were a prerequisite for health and possibly also for happiness, and I suspected they believed if the arches of your feet were not flat all would be well for you in all other aspects of your life. As eight- or nine-year-old boys, we had no choice but to put up with these arch supports. Later we managed to avoid wearing them.

I recall Dr. Scholl's arch supports were at one time readily available in New York City and were widely advertised. Susie and Ilse concluded from this, or rather seemed to have the attitude, that Americans were getting smarter as they seemed to have developed an appreciation for arch supports. In addition to concern that we not develop "fallen arches," my mother in particular set great store in "walking properly." She liked to walk behind me when we went for a walk and then make suggestions, the general nature of which was to move from the heel and roll forward onto the toes and then step off into the next step. The word she used was the German word "abrollen", somewhat equivalent to "stepping off" in English but with more emphasis on the rolling, and the "ab" is hard to translate as it has the sense of forcefully moving forward. My sister and I have admitted to each other that neither of us believes that our mother ever thought we got it quite right. I too did not believe I ever appreciated the concept with all the "finesse" that was implicit in my mother's devotion to "abrollen"—until recently, when a superb salesman in a shoe store explained in detail to my wife the superiority of some new, very fashionable and fairly expensive shoes with soles that were rounded so one rolled as one walked on them. Suddenly I had an epiphany: he's describing "abrollen." My mother would have been pleased; finally I "got it."

CHAPTER 42:

Ilse and Her Brother and Sister-in-Law, and Gatherings in Their Home in Scarsdale

My mother adored her brother, which is a credit to them both, especially as their relationship did not begin in the most auspicious way. My uncle did not welcome the arrival of another sister when my mother was born. He was four years old at the time, and felt that having an older sister Susie, who was two years older than him, was bad enough, and that another sister would be intolerable; at age four he had to be watched when the new baby arrived, as he had threatened to throw it out the window. (This is not hearsay; my uncle told me this himself and more than once.) But later in life he and my mother were close. I recall being with my mother and stopping off in Henry's office on 42nd Street in the mid 1940s on his fortieth birthday, to congratulate him on turning forty. Henry was always proud that he had rescued his little sister from Beirut and a "bad marriage," and that he had come to Beirut at his mother's request to help. What was done at Oma's behest was always viewed as having been done as though by some imperial command, as his mother was revered by her son.

As a former prosecutor Henry also had mastered the prosecutorial sense of righteousness and did not question that he had done something essential and of benefit when he rescued his sister. I believe my mother's divorce was the only divorce case he ever worked on in a legal capacity, and he was not cognizant of the more subtle aspects of family or divorce law. I am certain he never was involved with a case of an infant's custody other than in 1938, when he came to separate me and my mother from Hans Preiss and Beirut. I am certain that when I was an infant no one ever considered I might someday have a few questions. My interests were not necessarily being neglected at the time, but they were never considered in any depth. At the time my mother was "rescued" at her mother's (and probably also her sister's) behest, I was an infant; what I thought did not count.

When I once said to my aunt Susie, "Your brother is not a psychologist," she looked at me as though I were stupid, with a questioning look that said that I, as a doctor, should have known better, and answered, "A psychologist? He has no idea," or "He has not the least inkling"—or rather now that I am concentrating on what were her exact words, I recall she said in German, "Er hat keine ahnung davon" (He has not a clue). Say whatever you like about Germanic bluntness and forthrightness, being matter-of-fact and straightforward is often commendable, admirable, and has definite advantages. Susie knew her brother well; they were on the phone together every morning that the stock market was open, and discussed their trades and investments daily for decades. But Susie did not hesitate to assess her brother's qualifications as a psychologically astute person as "nil." "Big sisters" can be a nuisance to their little brothers, but they do know their little brothers.

Henry/Hans had been a lawyer in Germany until 1933 and was helpful to my mother and me with our immigration problems in the early 1940s, when Ilse and I arrived in the USA on a "tourist visa." He helped my mother become a U.S. citizen. In the early 1940s, Henry would pick up my mother and me whenever we came back from a vacation; my mother said to me when I was five years old that her brother liked to be helpful and share in people's adventures. He liked welcoming us back from our vacation to hear how we had liked wherever we had been. Perhaps Henry also wanted to hear about his sister's social life while on vacation and was hoping to hear that she had met a man she liked.

In 1985, the cooperative apartment that I had bought in 1977 for $85,000 had to be sold according to the terms of the divorce agreement that had been worked out between me and my first wife. That apartment had been bought using the money, or rather some of the money, Karl and Ilse had given me in 1977 on the advice of Paul, Karl's brother and lawyer. So my mother was inclined to view this apartment as one that she and Karl had bought for us, on the theory that without their financial help, it would not have happened. It is true that I would not have been able to buy that apartment had I not had their financial help. My mother and all concerned were impressed by the enormous increase in value of that apartment in just a few years. It was sold for $685,000 in 1985. My mother could not help telling her brother about this. It really was none of his business, but there always remained a deep-seated, unconscious desire in my mother that was due to a sentiment that I can only describe as being approximately analogous to the following: "You are my big brother and you think I know nothing about money, and you and Susie spend all your time investing in the stock market and do not think discussing business matters with me is worthwhile; but look how successful my son has been investing in real estate. You

should be impressed. Moreover, you should take me seriously." But little sisters stay little sisters.

I sympathize with my mother's deep-seated need to
impress her brother. I was surprised that I too was susceptible to such a desire to impress my uncle, and can therefore
empathize with my mother. When Henry was quite elderly, I
visited him one day for lunch at the Osborne Nursing Home
in Rye, New York, where he and several of his Scarsdale
neighbors were living. Both my mother and Henry's wife,
my aunt Margot, were dead by then. For some reason my
uncle asked me to come up to his room. There I saw he was
wrestling with some insurance papers written in German. He
explained that there was some German insurance policy that
might pay some of his wife's considerable medical expenses
incurred towards the very end of her life, but the forms
were long and complicated and all in German. I said that
as Margot had a taxable estate and would owe estate taxes,
and as the medical expenses at the end of her life were all tax
deductions from the estate, those expenses might not be so
bad as they would be heavily discounted. Henry was elderly,
but he was still witty and mentally sound; however, I was sad
to find that he had not thought of this, the first and only sign
I ever detected that he was not quite what he used to be in
business or financial matters. I think he was surprised I had
brought this to his attention, and he also was embarrassed he
had not yet thought of this himself. The next day he called
me to say, "Peter, you earned your lunch yesterday." And I felt
pleased that I had shown my uncle that I knew something he
had missed. He was then ninety-five or ninety-six, and I was
sixty-one or sixty-two. But I also thought to myself: "I am
being just like my mother; I am trying to impress my uncle
with my financial sagacity," which was silly as I have limited
skill in finance.

I was not nearly as close to Henry Samton as was my

cousin Albert, for whom Henry was like a father. Albert's own father, my uncle Ernst who died in 1967, was a medical doctor and had no interest in lawyers, or in law, which he thought was boring and petty. He once said to me he had no idea why Albert went to law school (at NYU). Ernst was too busy to be close to his son, or Susie was so possessive of Albert that Ernst did not intervene or compete for Albert's attention. So Albert was not close to his father. I liked Ernst, who liked me. Perhaps Ernst took some credit for himself or surmised he had influenced me to go to medical school, or liked to think so. He may have been partially right. Towards the end of his life Ernst and I were especially close. He had arranged for me to do minor surgery on homebound patients of his in 1965, when I was a surgical intern at Bellevue. Ernst and I traveled around Queens together and he introduced me to his patients as his nephew, a young surgeon. He no longer did minor surgery, as he was too nearsighted by then to sew stitches. We also occasionally went to afternoon theater matinees together, which he enjoyed and attended for the brief time between his retirement and his death.

Ernst had had a serious heart attack in the 1960s and had asked me to look at his cardiogram. He himself did not know how to interpret cardiograms. I gulped when I saw it; it was the worst EKG I had ever seen, showing a posterior wall infarct, an anterior wall infarct, and conduction disturbances—i.e. the stimulation and pathway of the electrical activity of the heart was abnormal and circuitous because so much of the heart had been damaged. I knew Ernst did not have much longer to live. Open-heart surgery and repair of occluded coronary arteries was not yet available then. The next time Ernst went to see the cardiology professor at NYU, he asked me to come with him. The doctor said to me, as Ernst was dressing in the examining room, "I am glad to see him again; I have not seen him in a while and I thought he might have died." No doubt this experienced doctor, who knew I was a young doctor as Ernst had introduced me as his nephew, a medical resident at Bellevue Hospital, was trying to tell me something. I do not doubt that Ernst took me along as he wanted someone to know and to share with him what he knew—that he was in trouble and had not much time left. Some months later, Ernst died.

Ernst had always been our family doctor. He took care of the medical problems of his extended family, but was not objective enough or removed enough to ever feel responsible for questioning the decisions that had been made for me and that had resulted in the banishment of Hans Preiss from my life. Ernst was not trained in psychiatry; he was a general practitioner and obstetrician by training. He also would not intrude in matters relating to my mother's personal life and to decisions which were supported by her family. I never was critical of my uncle Ernst, as he had taken care of me often. I respected him; I had recovered from many minor illnesses and such serious problems as hepatitis and appendicitis while under his care.

Albert often drove his uncle Henry up to Boston, where he saw a specialist in eye diseases and glaucoma in particular. I avoided getting involved with caring for Henry and only discussed things with him if he consulted me. After his mother died, Albert replaced her as Hans's confidant and discussed what to do in the stock market every day with his uncle Henry, and that drew them together. Albert knew a lot about his uncle's investments. After Margot died, Albert went up to the Osborne Nursing Home frequently. I went on occasion, or if Albert's wife, Susanne, called and said it was time for me to pay Henry a visit. I would go for lunch on Sundays. Henry was a good raconteur, and various elderly people who wanted to join us had to be waved away. Some old ladies made rather sour faces when my uncle said, "My nephew is visiting me today and we have things to discuss." What drew us together was my mother, who had been dead for some years. My uncle reminded me of my mother as he had similar facial expressions, a similar accent when speaking in English, and used similar verbal expressions and made similar gestures. (Jeanette, my wife, occasionally remarks to me, "You look or are making a facial expression just like your Uncle Hans.") Getting to see these facial expressions and mannerisms so reminiscent of my mother made it worth the effort to visit my uncle at the Osborne Nursing Home. Henry benefited in a reciprocal manner because I reminded him a lot of my mother.

My mother and her sister-in-law Margot Samton were friends. They both were often irritated by the close family that was centered in Jackson Heights. For Margot, the constant presence of her sister-in-law Susie was an annoyance. But Henry depended on his sister, who had introduced him to his business partner Herman Miltenberg and who also had provided money which had been needed to start his business. Henry used to say, "Without Susie and help from her *geht es uberhaupt nicht*" ("without Susie it does not work at all"; "*Es geht nicht*" is the German equivalent of the French "*Il ne marche pas*," meaning "it does not work"). My mother as well as Margot were shut out of the financial and business dealings that preoccupied Henry and his sister Susie. So Margot and Ilse shared a friendship and a bond, which included some annoyance at being minor players in business and financial matters relative to Susie and Henry. Ilse at times claimed she had saved her brother's marriage, but I doubt that she did more than listen to Margot when Margot had things to complain about and then make suggestions to her brother. My mother differed from Margot in that my mother could entertain people and cook meals for many people readily, and she valued making it seem easy. She often said that if the dinner party does not seem to have come together easily, the guests are not comfortable. We even used to say Ilse could give a dinner party for six people on an hour's notice. Margot found it harder to entertain people, but did more entertaining of family than did my mother.

Years ago I had no sympathy and less empathy with Hans Preiss. That changed. I also had little empathy for my uncle. When my grandmother died in 1970, I was surprised that her son was so upset. I did have some sympathy for my uncle at that time. I was a young doctor, and that a man in his sixties should be so distraught when his mother, who had been ill for some time and was in her eighties, died seemed strange or immature to me. I no longer feel that way; I was distraught when my mother died in 1997, when I was fifty-nine. So nothing is so certain; one learns or is forced to experience that one has more in common with other people than one had imagined, or in some instances, one has more in common than one would have liked or than one likes to acknowledge.

In the last two years of my mother's life (1995-1997), she often wanted to go out to Scarsdale. I would offer to drive her. I joked in those days—and it was not just a joke but was also to some degree a conclusion, based on my own experience— that my mother loved me, but she loved me the most when I was serving as her chauffeur. I soon found out it was best to schedule these visits to Scarsdale two weeks in advance. This then gave my mother some entertainment for the next two weeks and would justify making frequent if not daily calls to Margot and Henry. First she spoke with Margot; should my mother and I come for lunch or in the afternoon? Could she bring something? What was the weather like in Westchester? Then after a day or two my mother might call me to say she heard there might be snow. Perhaps we should not make the trip at all? When should we leave to avoid the traffic? Then a day or two before this event my mother would call me again to say she did not want to stay too long; perhaps it was not worthwhile to go out at all? Sometimes she would call and say Henry or Margot or she herself did not feel up to a visit on the day that had been scheduled. When I arrived to pick her up my mother often kept me waiting; she did not like how she looked and needed to change and wear something else. Once we arrived, Henry, Margot, and Ilse greeted each other affectionately and effusively. We then had a nice time chatting or inspecting the garden. We seldom stayed more than two hours. When she got into the car for the ride home my mother always said, "I am glad we came, but maybe we stayed too long." She was always glad to get back to her home. The next day I always received a call saying that she had enjoyed it, and that she had spoken to her brother or to Margot and they too had enjoyed the visit, and thanked me for having been the chauffeur.

Once my uncle moved to Scarsdale from Jackson Heights in 1952, visits there on holidays for family get-togethers were a regular part of our life. For at least twenty or twenty-five years, Thanksgiving was in Scarsdale. When I had my own family I preferred not to go there. My mother objected when I did not join her family in Scarsdale and sometimes tried to insist that I should drive her and Karl out there, say hello, stay a while and then return home. She did not like it when I said, "I do not want to drive on Thanksgiving if I can avoid it. Just take the train. They can pick you up from the train station there." For twenty or twenty-five years we always saw the Goldhabers, who drove in from Brookhaven to join the family gathering in Scarsdale. My mother explained to me that she and her siblings were the only family the Goldhabers had nearby. (Maurice's sister was in Israel, his brother was in California, and Trude's sister was in Rio de Janeiro.) On these occasions my mother would chat with Maurice, who was already then an eminent nuclear physicist and the chief administrator of Brookhaven National Laboratory, and would discuss with him what to do about the Russian physicists and the state of Russian atomic bomb development. My mother had some ideas of her own and did not hesitate to make some suggestions to Maurice. After the cold war was over (December 8, 1991, when the Soviet Union no longer existed) and the threat of trouble due to Russian Communism had abated, I said to my mother one day that I was glad the cold war was over. I added that now she no longer needed to give advice to Maurice Goldhaber on how to manage the Russian physicists and the atomic weapons program in Russia. Then, perhaps somewhat foolishly, I added what I thought was a realistic and objective comment that was not meant to be deprecating: "All that advice you gave Maurice over the years at our Thanksgivings probably is not what led to the demise of the Soviet Union." Ilse did not yield the least bit; she snapped back, "You cannot be so sure, though, can you?"

My mother particularly liked Michael Goldhaber, the younger of her cousin's two sons. He was a very thin young man, somewhat sickly at times from asthma, and looked more like his mother than did his brother. Ilse said he reminded her very much of how his mother had looked when she was young. He had various projects, and when he published a book, of which I saw one or two, there was always mention in the acknowledgements of gratitude for financial help from Karl and Ilse Schrag. Karl was on good terms with the Goldhabers, but the idea of giving Michael financial support undoubtedly came from my mother.

My cousin Albert never warmed up to the Goldhabers. He called them "freeloaders." When I told Ilse that her nephew Albert had referred to the Goldhabers as "freeloaders," my mother became truly obnoxious. She said it was perfectly O.K. to be a bank inspector (that's what Albert did) and it was O.K. to have nothing in one's head but information about stocks and bonds and derivative trading, but he had no idea what it meant to be an imaginative creative scientist. She said her cousins Trude and Maurice were far more interesting, contributed a great deal more to the world, and were also far smarter than Albert could begin to understand. Ilse said that they could hold their own with the world's leading scientists and were a national asset if the Russians got nasty and rattled nuclear weapons, and that Albert was a fool. But Albert was no fool; he may have had some resentment that Maurice and Trude always took his mother to fund raising dinners for the Weizmann Institute of Science in Israel, of which the Goldhabers were supporters and trustees. My aunt's respect and enthusiasm for the work of the Weizmann, and Maurice's recommendation to give some of her estate to the Weizmann, might very significantly reduce the size of his mother's estate and the size of Albert's inheritance. My aunt had occasion-ally discussed her enthusiasm for supporting the Weizmann with me when she came to see me as a patient in my office. I never knew exactly what to make of her ruminations about her will as she enjoyed entertaining numerous possibilities as to where to donate her money. She occasionally said she did not want to leave too much money to Albert, her only child. Once she explained, "If my daughter-in-law survives my son and gets a second husband with my money, I would turn over in my grave." Albert had some reason to be wary of these relatives, who were trying to get his mother to be a benefactor of the Weizmann Institute. Albert thought they were *schnorrers* (beggars or money raisers) or scroungers .

The physicists speak of light being both a wave and a particle at the same time, a concept rather hard to under-stand. But duality is common. A duality of apparently contradictory traits in the same person is quite common. The Goldhabers were demanding, and at times so intrusive that one had to consider whether it might not be best to avoid them altogether. Yet they were also generous, insightful, and respectful of my intelligence; they never underestimated my mathematical ability, and were able to challenge me to use my mathematical skills to deal with interesting and unusual problems. Having great scientists with original ideas in the family and consorting with them was intellectually demanding. Even when it seemed disadvantageous to be attentive to their demands, it was hard to resist Maurice and Trude. They had sophisticated and fanciful ideas. They influenced me and I respected them.

My grandmother was not a fan of the Goldhabers. She was Trude's aunt. My grandmother was not an intellectual, but she was clever and shrewd and did not hesitate to say to me one day, "The Goldhabers are too smart for their own or anyone else's good." After she said this to me, I discussed this with my mother, who explained that my grandmother was bitter over the death of her brother and his wife, thought this could have been avoided, and thought Trude and her sister had foolishly encouraged their parents to return from Switzerland to Munich to sell their house in the late 1930s, whereupon Otto and Nellie Scharff were apprehended and imprisoned and later were killed. My mother did not agree at all with her mother in regard to her cousin Trude Goldhaber, whom she respected and loved. My mother was aware that her cousin was a renowned theoretical physicist whose work on neutron decay was so critically important for the making of atomic bombs in the 1940s that it was classified as secret and could not be published. My mother also knew these distinguished theoretical physicists needed and appreciated help with the more practical details of life. Trude appreciated that my mother had been her friend, that I had been helpful to her and her children in my time at Harvard, and that my parents' home had always been available to her and Maurice as their home away from home when they came to New York City .

Trude and my mother knew they could count on each other as my cousin Albert and I knew we could always count on one another.

Without any question, my mother was an intellectual snob. She respected her physicist cousin and liked her cousin Eva Sheldon, who had been a secretary to Paul Rosenberg, the director and owner of an important art gallery in New York City. Karl too liked Eva, who had a genuine interest in painting and art. For many years she was a regular guest for supper in our home. But Ilse did not think highly of her cousin Rita Marschall, who was ten years younger than my mother. I once invited Rita and her husband Fred for afternoon tea at my home. My mother heard about it, called me, and said, "Rita and Fred are O.K. for the Brunells but not for you. If you are dumb enough to spend your time with her I will be disappointed in you." I called them off—not because I necessarily agreed with my mother, but it was silly to antagonize her in regard to her family. But years later, in 2007, when I was attending my cousin Albert's funeral, Albert being the first (and so far at least the only one) of my cousins to die and the first family member of my generation to die, Rita came up to me, saw I had been crying, and said, "I am surprised to see that you, Peter, are crying." I had been close to Albert; why should I have not been crying? Dumb: my mother was right on target once again.

Rita's husband Fred worked for forty years for my uncle and his partner, Herman Miltenberg, in their importing and exporting business. When Fred turned eighty I went at my mother's request to his birthday party. She liked Fred and said he deserved a lot of credit for being able to work for her brother and Herman Miltenberg for forty years. She thought I should go too, no doubt somewhat influenced by the fact that she and Karl needed me to drive them to this party. I also recall that we, Jeanette and I, went to Rita's seventieth birthday party in 1990, and we enjoyed it. Some of the respect that the Marschalls earned and deserved was due to the fact that they lived in the apartment directly next to that of my grandmother and, until 1969, when my grandmother no longer could live alone, were on the whole very kind and helpful to her. At that party I saw a woman named Ann Miltenberg, the daughter of my uncle's partner. My mother greeted her and said to this woman, by then in her forties, "You were supposed to marry my son, Peter." I cringed. In my family one never knows what manipulations and machinations are being plotted without consulting the children who will be affected and snared. Ann Miltenberg did not represent a threat or hazard to me in 1990, or ever, as far as I knew. But the mere possibility of hidden plots, or perhaps a whole minefield of such traps and schemes of which I was unaware, was exceedingly unpleasant and even "scary." It was the calm matter-of-fact way my mother referred to this scheme, as though it might have worked with no further need for elaboration, that was chilling even though the idea was ridiculous.

CHAPTER 43:

My Mother Foresees Problems and Tries to Protect Me with Some Advice

In 1964 I told my mother and father I was going to be an intern at Bellevue Hospital. "Do you think you know enough about these people and how they play?" asked my mother when I told her that I would be on the Columbia University Division. "These are very educated people, they are all Columbia professors." "I know what I am doing," I replied. "Besides, what does a simple woman like you know about academic medicine?" I added quite foolishly. My mother was annoyed and said, "Don't get fresh with me, young man. I had better call my friend, Dr. Andre Cournand. You will admit he knows something about academic medicine." So I admitted Dr. Cournand (Nobel Laureate in Medicine in 1956, and Professor of Medicine at Columbia University and Director of the Cardiovascular Research Laboratory at Bellevue) knew something about academic medicine as well as something about Columbia, and my mother called him. They spoke in

French. My mother had lived in Lebanon from 1933 until 1938 when she was married to Dr. Hans Preiss. My mother had learned French and spoke French in Lebanon, where she had socialized with French colonials. Karl had lived in Paris for some years and also spoke French. Ruth Fabian, Andre Cournand's secretary and, by 1964, his wife for quite some time, had lived in Paris and, while there in the 1930s, had been in Karl's circle of friends. My parents and the Cournands socialized together in New York City and when they were together they preferred to speak French.

When my mother reached Dr. Cournand she said, "My son has a tendency to get involved with things he does not need to get involved with. I have one question about Professor Ragan, the Director of the Columbia Division at Bellevue: Is he capable of appreciating my son without taking advantage of him?" Dr Cournand replied, "Absolutely. Tell your son that if there is one honest man in academic medicine who can be trusted, it is Dr. Ragan. Tell your son from me that he should trust him." My mother repeated to me what Dr. Cournand had said to her and I said, "You cannot expect me to do better than that. You see, I know what I am doing." My mother replied, "We shall see if you know what you are doing, we shall see." (To her credit my mother tried to inform and protect me and knew me and my liabilities well, and was far better at protecting me than almost anyone else; but I often resented this as being perhaps interfering or too overprotective. I knew I needed to be my own person and was vaguely aware I needed to get away from her "protection.")

Implicit in this conversation are some nuances and complexities that suggest how complicated my dealings with my mother actually were. Firstly, it was foolish for her to interfere with my work. I wanted some independence and privacy. Secondly, she did know things I possibly did not, but her protectiveness was not welcome. Thirdly, there was mistrust between my mother and me—not about her overprotectiveness, but about her views of doctors; and I knew, either consciously or unconsciously, that I needed to get beyond her limited respect or understanding of doctors. Fourthly, although my mother had insight into me and my vulnerabilities, she did not understand academia; academics are privy to knowledge that others do not have. My comment that she was "a simple woman" was intended to say that she did not have "academic" qualifications. I expressed it in a way that annoyed my mother, and had done so on purpose, as I was annoyed by her interference in my affairs. Yet she knew quite a lot about doctors, had been divorced from a doctor, and had hated aggressive and sleazy doctors, whom she had observed in Beirut. But I wanted to work for a good doctor/teacher and trust in my own judgment. If I learned to understand the psychology of doctors and to empathize with my absent biological father, or if I could partially reconstruct what had happened in 1938, that might be helpful to me.

I must admit that my mother was correct in many ways; she knew more about me than did anyone else, and correctly appraised Dr. Ragan whom she had never met and whom she would never meet. I would get into a fight some eight to ten years later that would alter my life, force me to leave the University, and lead to many changes. Even now I support the position I took in 1964—not because it was "correct," nor do I maintain it was "correct," whatever that means in a complicated professional environment, but because it was the only way I could solve my personal problem—and would make the same choices again. I actually still think that Dr. Ragan was one of the most decent, intelligent, kindly, and interesting persons I ever knew. He was a Catholic socialist by inclination. He was skilled at understanding young doctors and what they needed to master to develop their careers. When it comes to treating sick people and setting policy for the training of doctors, I believe he was more humane and his ideas were more suitable and appropriate than the Jewish right-wing doctors who believed "the purpose of being a doctor is to get rich." Because of my belief in a less mercenary approach to doctoring, I was deemed a pariah by some of my colleagues. My mother's premonition was absolutely correct; I did get badly beaten up in a nasty fight, but I like to think I retaliated as roughly and as effectively as I received.

Some years ago I had a conversation by phone with my daughter. She said she was busy collecting letters of recommendation and support for her being promoted to be a full professor of medicine at Harvard Medical School. I asked—not entirely seriously—if she wanted a letter of support from me; I was after all certified by the American College of Internal Medicine and was a Fellow of the American College of Physicians. She answered that she needed letters from important people ("I need letters from more important people than you, Dad") who published papers, ran clinical labs, and had large and long bibliographies referring to their work. I said, "No matter how many papers these people have published or however big their labs may be, I have known you better and longer than they have, and could write a far better and more informative letter than they can. But don't worry, daughter. I have no intention of writing a letter about you and never had; and good luck." I had learned something my mother did not believe in and did not support: business is business and family is family, and they should be kept separate if at all possible. Unfortunately, in my family that did not work. I never got away from being under the influence of my prominent relatives, who thought academic medicine was pretentious and of no scientific merit. They viewed the intellectual and scientific pretensions of medical doctors as completely ridiculous. Even worse, they were angry and annoyed about the pretentiousness of those who were incompetent in math and physics. Gertrude Goldhaber advised me in the early 1980s, when I was at the Columbia Presbyterian Medical Center, to "just get out of that institution."

In 1964 or early in 1965 I was on vacation in Opalocka, Florida, with my family visiting my parents-in-law. At approximately 2:30 p.m. the phone rang. It was an administrator in Washington, D.C., calling to offer me a job as an Epidemic Intelligence Officer with the Communicable Disease Center in Atlanta. They had my name as I had applied for a job in the U.S. Public Health Service. These positions were acceptable in lieu of military service, and by getting such a job I could and would avoid going to Viet Nam or the military. The administrator complained that it had been hard to reach me. I thanked him for his efforts. What had happened is that he had called Bellevue Hospital and had learned I was on vacation. The departmental secretary referred him to my parents who happened to be home. Then he reached my mother and explained to my mother why he was calling, that the job would be in Atlanta starting in July 1966, and that the urgency in reaching me was because I would have to accept the offer by 4:30 p.m. that afternoon. My mother said she had my number in Florida, that I might or might not be in, and thought that this was a ridiculous request. In no way would I consider moving to Atlanta and/or decide to do so in the next two hours. She thought this was a nuisance call. The administrator said he had to argue with my mother for a while before she gave him my number. He phoned me—fortunately I was near the phone—and I accepted the position, and I avoided military service by working as a U.S. Public Health Service Officer from 1966 to 1968. Fortunately my mother had decided, as she explained to me when we discussed this phone call, that she should probably not interfere in my business affairs.

CHAPTER 44:

North Carolina in 1966, Occupational Health, and Leftist Sympathies— Both Mine and My Mother's

In 1966 I was living in Raleigh, North Carolina. I worked at the State Health Department and was a Lt. Commander in the U.S. Public Health Service on loan to the State Health Department in North Carolina. Daniel was a baby and Deb was just two years old. Karl and Ilse came down for a weekend and, after a day or two in Raleigh where we showed them our apartment and the place where I worked, we headed off to the Carolina coast near Morehead City and the beautiful beaches there. Morehead City now has a population of about eight thousand people; in 1966 it was less than half that. It is about halfway on the North Carolina coastline, i.e. from Morehead City, Virginia to the north is as far away along the coastline as is South Carolina to the south. We had a good time at the beach for a day or two and were heading back to Raleigh; we were somewhere in Eastern Carolina. It was a very hot day. I was driving a new white Plymouth Valiant, a four-door sedan that had cost $2,100 and which my parents had given me as a present, and which we had bought just before driving to Raleigh. With my family and my parents in the car the Valiant seemed crowded.

At a gas station we stopped for gas and bought some bottles of water and Coca-Cola. (Coca-Cola is made in Atlanta and has Southern roots, and we drank lots of it while living in the South.) Just a bit earlier Ilse had asked us if we had made any friends yet, and we had said we had not yet found any. As we were getting back into our car, we saw another couple with two young girls getting out of their car. The man called to his wife in German. This was too intriguing for my mother to pass up. She went over and introduced herself to them and started a conversation. Ilse then asked where they lived. They said Knightdale, which is just ten miles east of Raleigh, and my mother then introduced us. That was our first meeting with Peter and Inge Witt. The friendship developed, and we saw Peter and Inge for many years thereafter and we were quite close friends. My kids liked visiting them at their Knightdale farm. (Knightdale had a population of two thousand then, but it is 28,000 by now.)

The chief of occupational health at the North Carolina Health Department, who asked me to travel with him and survey some problems, is the person who got me involved with occupational lung disease in North Carolina. But without question occupational lung disease and oppressive working conditions affecting (mostly) white textile workers had political implications, and my somewhat leftist sympathies did affect my reaction to what I found and what I then decided to do to improve matters. Were my parents partially responsible for my views because of their socialist sympathies? Perhaps. I was not brought up to be an aggressive moneymaker. When I was a boy, Ilse had always recommended that I be "hubsch,

nett, und bescheiden" (look nice, be friendly, and be modest).
The first time I wondered if my home was significantly politically different from others was when I was in eighth grade
at Public School #6 and said in history class to my teacher,
Ms. Margerie Lewis, that the Russians helped defeat the
Germans in the second world war, only to be angrily reprimanded by my teacher: "The USA won the Second World
War—the Russians only helped to fight Japan five days before
the war was over; don't get me started on that." (In Berlin
there is a memorial to the thirty thousand Russian soldiers
who died in the last days of the Second World War in the
battle to subdue and conquer Berlin, which we saw when we
were in Berlin some years ago. I thought of Ms. Margerie
Lewis and eighth grade when I saw it).

Before then I never thought I had to be careful and say
only what was acceptable or politically correct. Nor had I
considered myself a "leftist," and I had never been prepared
to be viewed as such. Friends of my parents included German
Jewish refugees with leftist sympathies, and during the 1950s
most people who came to our home had opposed Senator
McCarthy and his "witch hunts" for traitors in government. When President Truman dismissed General Douglas
MacArthur in April 1951 for "insubordination" ("with deep
regret I have concluded that General of the Army, Douglas
MacArthur, is unable to give his wholehearted support to the
policies of the United States Government and of the United
Nations in matters pertaining to his official duties"—President Truman), Karl and Ilse suggested I miss school that
April morning rather than go with my eighth grade class
and school to greet General MacArthur and wave flags at his
motorcade in Central Park as was planned and ordered by
the school principal. Ilse did not like using school children
to wave flags at a parade honoring a general (and an insubor-
dinate one at that); she had seen children used to wave flags

in Berlin in support of Hitler and "National Socialism" in the early 1930s.

When I went to Oxford with Fran in 1955 we visited Nicholas Kurti (1908-1998), a professor of low-temperature physics at Oxford University and a close friend of our family. Kurti was Jewish, had been born in Hungary, and had a Ph.D. in physics from the University of Berlin (1933), but had moved to England in 1933. He had been close to Dori Furth and had proposed marriage to her, but she had turned him down. (This information was recently corroborated for me by Francis Schrag.) I once read in a biography of Klaus Fuchs that the only physicist in the West who maintained ties with Klaus Fuchs (1911-1988), the spy for the Russians who had stolen atomic secrets from Los Alamos while working for the British as a physicist in the early 1940s, was Nicholas Kurti. Kurti and Fuchs were close in age; they were friends and colleagues, both had fled from Nazi Germany to England in 1933, and both had worked at Los Alamos. I recall discussing Kurti's visiting Fuchs in East Germany, where Fuchs lived after being released from jail by the British, with my parents in the 1960s. They reminded me that Fuchs had been prosecuted and jailed in England for giving away classified information, not for being a traitor. "Treason" in English law signifies and requires that one has aided the enemy. Fuchs was not tried for "treason," as the Russians were our allies fighting with the British and the Americans against a common enemy when Fuchs was sending them information from Los Alamos.

My mother and her cousin belonged to a Jewish Socialist Youth movement when they were nineteen-year-old students at the University of Freiberg in 1929-1930, and this had left my mother with leftist sympathies. That was almost a decade before I was born, and at a time when all Europeans had to choose between the hard right or the anti-Fascist "left." Was

I somewhat influenced by my mother's past political inclina-
tions? No doubt I was. But the more significant influence on
my professional life were my mother's physicist cousins. They
were definitely leftist in their sympathies, were dedicated to
using their scientific and administrative skills to restructure
institutions so they were less right-wing, and did not hesitate
to recruit or use me to further their interests. These included
scientific education and institutional fundraising. They had
leftist tendencies as they were refugees from Hitler's Germany. Trude received her Ph.D. in physics *summa cum laude*
from the university of Munich in 1935, but almost did not
get her degree. She was accused of having been disrespectful
to Minister Joseph Goebbels in that she did not stand up to
salute him at the end of his address when he spoke at the
university. But the accuser, the Dean (or Chancellor), did not
know that some weeks previously an edict had been passed
stating that the Jews should remain seated. Trude pointed
this out to the Dean (or Chancellor), he verified that she was
correct, and then said with a smile, according to Trude, that
she therefore would get her degree after all; he had been
mistaken. After she told me this little anecdote I remarked,
"No wonder you are a little leftist."

She had additional reason to be on the left; her parents
were apprehended and allegedly were to be transferred by
train to Latvia, but were executed along with a thousand
others before the train arrived in Latvia. This aunt and uncle
of my mother's were the only family my mother lost due to
the Nazis. My mother said she had been close to Gertrude's
parents, her uncle Otto and her aunt Nellie, but her brother,
my uncle Henry Samton, had been closer. Otto Scharff had
pressured my uncle Henry to choose, when he was in his early
twenties, between the two young women he was intimate
with at the time and limit himself to one woman. Henry
took his uncle's advice and chose Margot, who would be his

wife and the mother of his three children. My uncle told me all this as we were driving together out to Bayport, Long Island, to celebrate Trude's eightieth birthday with Maurice and Trude in July of 1991.

The late 1960s was an exciting time to be in North Carolina. I opposed the Viet Nam war. Prominent leaders, both black and white, debated the advisability of joining the anti–Viet Nam war movement to the civil rights movement, and the concept of "private property" was used or had recently still been used to justify oppressive working conditions, segregated restaurants, segregated parks (as in Winston-Salem, where Reynolds Park did not admit any "colored"), and segregated hospitals and nursing homes. "Unions" were anathema to management, to the point that every few months an (alleged) union organizer was found lying dead with a knife in his back near some textile mill. My secretary in 1966, a lovely young local woman, on hearing I paid our black nanny a dollar per hour, said "Why, Dr. Schrag, that is way too much. For that you could hire a white man." My boss, a shrewd observer of local sentiment and politics, warned me one day, "When you meet with the president of the local medical society in that county, Peter, I want you to remember that in that rural county the homes have private wells from which they get their water. A public water supply system has been repeatedly voted down on the grounds that it is a form of 'communism.'" I recall saying only, "Oh." In those days there were billboards along the highway in Eastern North Carolina saying, "Impeach Earl Warren." It was easy to be a little on the left in North Carolina in the 60s.

CHAPTER 45:

Artist Friends

My mother always gave small dinner parties without any help. One of Karl's friends who was a frequent guest was a man named Tom Young. He was an art professor as well as the museum director at Wagner College on Staten Island. He had Karl lecture there, and Karl had a small show there once. Sabine Gova, an old friend, also a European refugee from both fascist Germany and Vichy France, with one Catholic and one Jewish parent, was employed at Wagner College as an art historian and lecturer. (She had a sister, her only sibling, named Ursula Filene, whose husband was Herman Filene, an important man in Ilse's and my life story in that he is the person who, in Berlin in 1931 or 1932, introduced my mother to Hans Preiss, a young doctor at the time. The Filene's son, Peter Filene, a professor of history at the University of North Carolina at Chapel Hill in adult life, was a year behind me at Friends. When we were in high school we took German lessons together one afternoon a week from Sabine Gova, his aunt.) Sabine Gova got the job at Wagner College via a recommendation from Karl, who knew Tom

Young. I remember that Tom Young always would bring a very attractive young woman along when he came to us for supper. These young women who came with Tom Young were always airline stewardesses. Sometimes he brought the same one several times, but we never saw the same stewardess more than three times. These women always jumped up and were helpful, and Ilse liked to invite Tom Young in part as she appreciated his helpful girlfriends who, as trained airline stewardesses, knew how to pick up dishes and help serve.

A couple who were both artists and also close friends of my parents and frequent guests in their home were Reuben and Gerry (Geraldine) Tam. She was the art teacher for years at the Dalton School, and he was a fine and interesting artist. They summered for one or two decades on Monhegan Island, an island twelve miles off the Maine coast, where my parents would occasionally visit them. They were natives of Hawaii, and in the 1960s or early 1970s they retired to Hawaii where they both had grown up. Thereafter no one who lived in New York and did not get to Hawaii ever saw them again. In the 1980s, Jeanette and I were going on vacation to Hawaii to the island of Kauai. Ilse and Karl said we had to look up the Tams. I had not seen them in years and my parents did not remember which island they had retired to almost two decades earlier. My mother was annoyingly insistent that we had to include seeing them on our trip. I explained that the Hawaiian Islands cover a vast expanse of territory and that there are multiple separate islands, and that visiting the Tams might not be so simple. Besides, Jeanette and I were going there on vacation, not to conduct a search for the Tams. Ilse was annoyed. I cannot say for sure that Karl was also annoyed, but I can say that Ilse's intense annoyance suggests that Karl too was annoyed and let Ilse speak for him, as was often the case. My mother was offended and felt insulted by my lack of interest in seeing their close friends. I explained we were flying to Kauai and that I would look up the Tams in the phone book once I arrived. If they were on that island we would certainly look them up. This mollified my mother somewhat; she was unfamiliar with Hawaii and accepted that the Hawaiian Islands were spread over the Pacific Ocean and that we might not find the Tams easily.

I never had expected to find the Tams on Kauai. But I wanted to keep my word, so shortly after checking into the Coconut Grove Hotel—now a defunct ruin, but then an elegant hotel where Elvis Presley had stayed when filming and starring in the movie *Blue Hawaii*—I looked up the Tams in the local phone book. They lived in a town called Kappa'a, which was just two miles up the road from our hotel. The Tams were happy to hear from us, and they knew me as I had had supper with them many times in my parents' home. We had a lovely afternoon together the following day. They had a large garden with exotic fruit trees and many unusual flowering plants native to Hawaii which they cultivated carefully. I was sorry my mother did not have a chance to see their garden as she would have appreciated it even more than we did. When we got back to New York we gave Karl and Ilse a full report on the Tam's house, garden, and studio, downplaying a bit that Reuben was not well. My mother was pleased that we had connected with these old friends.

CHAPTER 46:

My Mother Finds Us an Apartment but Fails to Keep Her Promise; I Make Good on Her Promise Years Later to Insure That She Kept Her Word

In 1968 we were leaving Raleigh to return to New York City. Finding a place to live was a problem. Ilse found us a two-bedroom apartment at 680 West End Avenue. It was a rent-controlled building owned by I.B. Simkowitz and managed by a German or Austrian Jewish woman, who was not young, named Ms. Wiener. Her assistant was Mr. Marty Cohen. Ilse said that we were a young family, that I was a young doctor who was still completing his residency, and no doubt we would not live there for long which made us attractive tenants for Ms. Weiner. Ilse explained to Mr. Cohen that Karl was an important artist and printmaker and that if he, Mr. Cohen, got us an apartment, she would give him a print. We lived there for nine years (1968-1977), and then moved to 90 Riverside Drive in 1977. In 1980 Ms. Wiener was helpful to me in that she also was the managing agent for two buildings on 110th Street, and found me an apartment at 515 West 110 Street. That was helpful at the time, as Ilse was more than a little annoyed that I had been living with her sister (on an emergency basis, as I had nowhere else to live that June) in Jackson Heights in my cousin Albert's old bedroom. Ilse disliked my living with her sister and my getting so involved at that stage of my life with Susie. I was glad that I could reassure my mother that Ms. Wiener had promised she would have an apartment for me by Labor Day, and Ms. Wiener came through for me. Years before, when we lived directly above Ms. Wiener, I would say to my kids when they were making noise that Mrs. Wiener would come up and scold them, thinking that, as Ms. Wiener terrified every tenant in her three buildings, she would also be able to frighten or intimidate my children. However, my daughter Deborah, no more than ten years old at the time, said she was not afraid of Ms. Wiener: "Anyway, Dad, she has a crush on you." My daughter is smart and observant, and perhaps her remark was helpful in that it later served to increase my confidence that Ms. Wiener would find me an apartment. In early September of 1980 I was living alone at 515 West 110th Street in a perfectly adequate small and somewhat modest apartment that Ms. Wiener had found for me. (Ms. Wiener moved me to a larger, better one in the same building a few months later.) Ilse was so happy that I was no longer living with her sister that she gave me a check for $5,000 to buy myself some furniture for my new apartment. But Ilse never came through on her promise to Marty Cohen.

By 1998 both Ilse and Marty Cohen had died. Mrs. Cohen was still living at 680 West End Avenue, around the block from me and Jeanette. I saw Mrs. Cohen on occasion as she and I both walked to the tennis courts in the park where we played tennis and sometimes our paths crossed. One day we spoke and I learned Marty had died, and she reminded me of my mother's promise. I did not doubt my mother had made it. I had more of Karl's prints than I knew what to do with, and picked out a large nice one and delivered it to Mrs. Cohen at 680 West End Avenue. The next time I saw Mrs. Cohen she graciously thanked me, said she liked it very much, and that it had been "worth the wait." I redeemed my mother's credibility, but it was more than thirty years between the time the promise was made and when Mrs. Cohen got that print.

CHAPTER 47:

Carrying Gifts of Comfort and Joy, as My Mother Instructed

When I was a teenager, or even before then, I would deliver Christmas or New Years gifts to my parents' friends who lived in Greenwich Village. Fred and Dorothy Farr lived in what was later Tribeca, Elizabeth Lunau lived with her daughter on Barrow Street, and Lilian Ben-Zion and Ben-Zion lived on Morton Street. These were all old and good friends. Lilian painted and Ben-Zion wrote, painted, and made sculptures. Fred Farr was a talented artist who painted, did sculpture, made leather shoes, designed and made jewelry, and was a talented ceramicist/potter. His first wife, Dorothy, painted large abstract paintings. She was an admirer of the work of Jackson Pollack. In the early 1950s Karl told me that, according to Dorothy Farr, Jackson Pollack would become a famous artist. Unfortunately for Kathy and me, Karl did not buy any Jackson Pollack paintings as Dorothy had recommended. Fred and Dorothy had bought an old one-room schoolhouse in Thomaston, Maine for about $200, when the

Hancock County school districts were being consolidated in the early 1950s; the one-room abandoned schoolhouses could then be bought for almost nothing. They drove over often from Thomaston to Friendship in an old car with a stick shift that rose up vertically from the floor of the car. I occasionally went with Fred to collect clay from some mud banks to use for his clay sculptures, which were then cast in bronze. Fred exhibited his work at the Paul Rosenberg Gallery on 79th Street just west of Madison Avenue, but his work in bronze, sculptures of armored horses such as those used in battle in ancient China, never became a hit with the public.

In the 1980s, my mother told me to see Fred Farr's show at a gallery in Tribeca. I bought a statue of an armored horse which stands on the living room coffee table in my home. As Fred helped me carry this heavy bronze statue of an armored horse to my car, he said he had sold two pieces from the show which had lasted several weeks and was about to end; one was bought by Karl, the other by me. A few years later Fred had lung cancer. My mother had the idea to apply to the Rothko Foundation, which was established to give financial aid to artists in need, and they gave a large grant to Fred. Karl told me he spoke at Fred's funeral. (I cannot remember why I did not attend; no doubt I was not in New York at the time.) Twenty years after Fred Farr died, his widow exhibited some of his work in a gallery in Soho in New York City. Jeanette and I went, and we admired some drawings. I priced some drawings which his widow said cost about $10,000 each. I said I loved them but that was more than I could afford to spend. We chatted and I introduced Jeanette and myself to Jane Farr, and she remembered me well, which could only have been from those visits at Christmas time when I delivered a gift. She said Fred would have wanted me to have one of those drawings; we settled on the very low price of $500, and I paid the $500 and took the drawing home. It now hangs in our living room. My mother would have taken (and in this case deserves) partial credit, as she had sent me on those errands to distribute gifts to her and Karl's friend.

Karl never used his knowledge of art or artists to invest in art. Art was his profession and interest, and was not something he did for investment purposes. To do so would create a conflict that would eventually be detrimental to his artistic judgment and purpose in life. Karl believed this, just as he believed it was impossible to support oneself as a commercial artist if one wanted to be a serious artist. Karl recommended to his friends to earn money as an art teacher or a framer, if necessary, but to avoid commercial art work which would eventually corrupt one's creative efforts. Although Karl did not buy art for investment purposes, he did collect works of art done by others. He bought what he liked on occasion and exchanged work with friends and colleagues whose work he admired. This same subtle distinction and consideration, not to engage in drawing for commercial or secondary purposes unrelated to the work itself, caused Karl to have reservations about the work of his extremely successful neighbor Al Hirschfeld, whose cartoons or caricatures of important figures in the theater world were on the front of the Theater Section of the *New York Times* every Sunday for many years. But Karl and Al liked and respected each other, attended each other's shows, and developed a friendship which I think was encouraged and reinforced by the fact that Dolly, Al's wife, and Ilse were friends and encouraged their husbands to show regard for one another and one another's work. Ilse and Dolly met regularly on 95th Street.

CHAPTER 48:

Ilse Had More Discretion Than Most People Imagined Her to Have

When his brother Paul consulted him as to which American artist did interesting work that he might buy, Karl recommended buying a Marsden Hartley painting. That was in the 1950s and Paul bought two Hartleys, each for less than $10,000. One he sold again a few years later, as he did not really like it. The other was a classic Hartley view of Mount Katahdin. It was hanging in Paul and Susie's home for years. It was sold a decade ago for over one million dollars. I recall visiting my aunt, by then a widow, in her apartment one day and I noticed that when we went out for a walk she did not lock the door to her apartment. She explained her eyesight was poor, and she could not unlock the door when she returned to her home as she could not find the keyhole. I called my cousin Raymond to say that the Hartley, which I had been told was now very valuable, could easily be taken and that he should be aware that the apartment was left unlocked.

Soon afterwards, the Hartley view of Mount Katahdin was sold. What I noticed is that my mother never mentioned or referred to or boasted of the financially successful recommendation that Karl had given them, which was of considerable benefit to his nephews. Ilse knew Karl was not investing in art, that he did not want to have anyone think he could or should invest in art, and she knew it would be very "gauche" to mention this. She knew the Schrag family were proud and private and would not approve of such an indiscretion. So never at any time as far as I know did either Karl or Ilse comment on the valuable Marsden Hartley that Karl had advised his brother to buy. Ilse had no difficulty telling her brother that my co-op apartment had sold for $680,000, which was none of his business and an intrusion into my affairs. But boasting of my financial coup and intruding into my affairs and financial situation to impress her brother, a businessman, was perfectly acceptable from my mother's point of view. She and Karl, after all, had provided us with the financial support that enabled us to buy that apartment. She imagined she deserved partial credit, and whether it was O.K. to intrude on my privacy was never a major consideration for my mother. I was her son, and Karl's privacy was one thing but mine need not be given the same consideration. I do not mean to suggest that this was conscious; it was an unconscious attitude. My mother's readiness to discuss the price of the co-op apartment I sold in 1985 is only mentioned here to highlight how remarkable and significant it was that never did Karl nor Ilse comment on how valuable the Hartley view of Mt. Katahdin had become and that Karl had been instrumental in Paul's getting it. I mention this as Ilse's discretion was not a quality she was given much credit for; she had a reputation for being outspoken, but, in fact, she had considerably more discretion than she was ever given credit for having.

My mother believed that women are more influential and important in the scheme of things than is acknowledged. She would have been greatly amused had I explained to her that I was involved with restructuring the financial remuneration for the medical doctors at the Columbia Presbyterian Medical Center. She would have recognized that this was essentially putting into effect the agenda of the Jewish Socialist Youth Movement she and her cousin had belonged to in 1929 when she was nineteen years old. This movement was dedicated to steering the institutions of Germany between the far right and the far left, as my mother's cousin explained to me in a letter she sent me in February of 1988. My mother had influenced me to be considerate of the problems of working-class people, and I was readily cognizant of the problems in the North Carolina textile industry. I was perceived by my mentor as a "Jewish Socialist" after giving my talk on Byssinosis in the North Carolina textile industry. He then used me as the head goat for new financial policies. Trude's husband was also involved in the administration of Columbia, as he had been consulted by the top administrator at Columbia. But I did not let my mother hear about the problems of Columbia and medical politics. She might have been amused but she also might get wrought up about "medical politics." In those days I did not want her to be involved or concerned with my work or my highly personal choices.

CHAPTER 49:

My Mother "Checks Up" on MetLife

I worked as a medical doctor for MetLife full time from 1988 to 2003. For a while I had an enormous office on the 16th floor in the MetLife building on 24th Street and Madison Avenue, with a huge desk that was a valuable antique, numerous windows, and a spectacular view over Madison Square Park. People who came to see me in that grandiose office would assume I was important just from the size of the desk and the office. My mother came by and was impressed. But the grandiose office was not to be mine for long. They moved us into the adjacent building and built us a department in the basement. My office there was small, with just enough room for me, a patient, and the large antique desk. My mother again came by and said, "No windows and you are in the basement. I would get another job." She appeared at MetLife occasionally as she was often on 23rd Street. She periodically went to the League for the Hard of Hearing, which was on 23rd Street near Sixth Avenue, and had her hearing aids fixed. Being nearby she could not resist stopping by to see me. As I was then in charge of our little clinic, my staff rushed to greet her, "the boss's mother," when she showed up and she enjoyed the welcomes she received from my nurses. She sometimes asked the nurses a question or two and they then reported to me about what she said. These visits were more fun for her than for me, but I felt it was more mature on my part to allow her to come than to prohibit her from coming.

One day I was at work and she called me. She said it was something urgent. I was worried that something had happened to her or Karl; but that was not the case at all. There was a sale at Bancrofts, a men's clothing store on Madison Avenue. A sale was on for jackets; Karl had bought one, and if I arrived there before 6:00 p.m., I could pick out a second jacket for just $60. I was relieved nothing more serious had happened. I left work in time to get to Bancrofts, and picked out a jacket. The saleslady said the sale required that I have the slip from the first jacket, the one Karl had already bought. I asked to see the manager. I explained that my mother had been in earlier with her husband, my father; I described him, and then said, "You remember serving them. Look at my face; was that my mother who was here earlier this afternoon with my father?" She looked at me, saw the resemblance to my mother, and said to the assistant, "Give him the sale price."

Karl and Ilse would sublet their brownstone in the summertime. Often they sublet it to students or young academics. In the 1980s they would quite blithely say, "If there are any problems, just call our son who lives on the West Side and he will handle it." I could not refuse to get involved, and there were problems that came at inconvenient times. One not particularly conscientious or bright young woman was repeatedly careless about turning off the burglar alarm and would set it off, forgetting how to turn the noise off. I had to rush up to 127 East 95th Street twice to turn off the deafening noise from the burglar alarm, as only I knew how to turn it off. I would not be surprised if the neighbors still remember these incidents. It was all eventually handled, but I recall being concerned every summer as to who the tenant would be and whether that person would be responsible. My mother just assumed I could and would handle whatever might come up without difficulty. She thought highly of my competence when it suited her purposes.

MetLife is a huge company and was also a major player in the New York City real estate market, as Metlife owned Peter Cooper Village and Stuyvesant Town in those days. Ilse would study the *New York Times* almost daily and, in the last decade of her life (1987-1997), would bring to my attention whenever bad publicity about MetLife appeared in the *Times*. Then she would ask if I was connected to whatever was being criticized and ask, "Are you sure you want to work there?" But I reassured her that I was never asked to do something that I really did not want to do, and said I was no more responsible for all the things MetLife did than a mailman would be responsible for all the things the federal government did. (Mailmen in those days were employees of the federal government.)

My mother liked to claim credit for some things that happened for which she did not deserve the credit. For years, Ilse claimed that the courtship of Bob and Carole Pesner and their marriage occurred because Bob and Carole admired a painting of Karl's that my mother had shown to them; then Bob bought it for Carole, and this led to their getting involved and married. There was never any reason for me to question this, although it was somewhat implausible that this was an accurate description of Bob and Carole's courtship. But one morning, many years later, the C.E.O. of MetLife, a Mr. Harry Kamin, came to see me. He was a second cousin of Carole Pesner. She was by then the owner and director of the Kraushaar Galleries (where Karl had exhibited his work for half a century) and had been the heiress of Antoinette Kraushaar. Harry Kamin told me he had one of Karl's prints in his home and that he had recently bought a painting from Carole. I explained I too had recently bought a painting from Carole and we chatted. I told him that Bob Pesner's mother, Fanny, had been my first patient in 1970 when I opened my office, and we discussed her as we both had known her well and she had been a very intelligent and interesting woman. Harry Kamin said Carole's son, Jonah Pesner, a rabbi, had officiated at his daughter's wedding recently. Then I mentioned my mother claimed credit for the courtship of Bob and Carole. Harry said, "Not at all; I introduced Bob to Carole and deserve credit for their getting married." I smiled and said I did not insist that my mother's claim was necessarily valid.

CHAPTER 50:

Living in Maine Without a Car

E xcluding four summers when they made trips to Italy,
Mexico, Colorado, and Spain, Karl and Ilse spent their
summers in Maine and rented places for the summer season
from 1945 to 1967. After Great Chebeaque Island in 1945,
they spent one summer at Spruce Head near Rockland,
one summer in Castine, two summers in Harborside/Cape
Rosier, four summers in Friendship, and two summers in
Vinalhaven, where they rented the home of their friend, the
artist Rafael Soyer. Never during all those years did they
have access to or drive a car. Karl liked to walk and com-
municate with nature and did not like getting into cars. Ilse
had a driver's license but never drove for twenty or thirty
years after she first got her license. We traveled to Maine on
the Bar Harbor Express, a train with Pullman service (i.e.
beds were made up and the train went through the night). At
Portland the train that originated in New York was broken
up and some railroad cars were shunted onto other tracks and
given another engine that would take them to Bangor, while
other cars were routed towards Rockland and the coast. The

delay in Portland took an hour at least; Ilse would get off the train to buy some drinks or sandwiches or a cup of hot tea for Karl, and I would always worry whether she would find her way back to the right railroad car after the rearranging of the train. She always said there would not be a problem, but sometimes another train separated our train from the station and I worried as to how she could get back if that train did not pull out of the station before ours did. I truly hated our stops in Portland and my mother's reassurances as she got off the train that she would be right back never convinced me. But she took this little ritual as a challenge and enjoyed it.

So for many years our two large trunks and a crate containing art supplies were sent ahead by Railway Express. While in Maine we depended on taxi drivers, local delivery service from the grocery stores, and rode bicycles. We were in Friendship for four summers when I was twelve to sixteen years old. I had a bicycle with a seat in the front and drove the three miles to town often. Just before getting to Friendship there was a steep hill that one went down and then another steep hill one had to go up. My sister Kathy would sit in the seat in front of me and hold on to the handle bars of the bike (she was three to five years old), and we would fly down the hill just before town. Helmets were unknown in those days. I still think we were safe. If I had to say when in my life I was closest to my sister, I would say on those bike rides going down that hill to Friendship, on the trip to Spain in 1958 when we would share a hotel room and she would be considerate of me and write in her diary in the bathroom so the light would not disturb me while I was sleeping, and when I was in high school when we shared a room with a large divider/screen. She slept while I sat at my desk and did homework. Once I left for college in September of 1955, when I was seventeen and she was seven, Kathy had the room to herself. I was relegated to Karl's print workshop whenever I was home from then on.

I think Ilse was less enthusiastic about living in Maine without a car as time passed. I was encouraged to get driving lessons from a man called Floyd when I was eighteen. He was a taxi driver on Vinalhaven. Floyd was also authorized to give me a driving test and, if I passed to his satisfaction, I was awarded a driver's license for the state of Maine. I recall that for a few months thereafter, and until I passed the driving exam in New York for the New York State driver's license, I used that Maine license to occasionally drive a friend's car. I also recall Floyd giving me my Maine license and telling me to be careful, adding that he personally only drove on the island of Vinalhaven. "Driving on the mainland around Rockland in all that traffic is far too crazy and dangerous for me," he said. He explained that he had tried driving on the mainland once and decided he would not attempt it ever again.

My mother encouraged me to have a car just before my third year of college, in 1957. She thought it would be good for me, and wanted to have me available to her when I was home on vacations to drive her and her mother around town and back and forth from Jackson Heights to my parents' home in Manhattan. My grandmother was driven around by my mother's sister Susie, and Ilse wanted to be able to offer her mother rides as did her sister. But I had a problem: my girlfriend from high school had followed me to the greater Boston area and would be in her second year at Wellesley College. She had stated clearly she wanted to be married by the time she finished college. I knew I should break off with her, although I still liked her. Our dating the previous year had been complicated by my not having a car to go out to Wellesley. She would be pleased if I owned a car, as then she could see me more often. I did not want to explain to my mother that owning a car created rather than solved problems for me, nor did I want to give her information about my private life, its problems, and my conflicting feelings, and the status of my involvement with this girlfriend. I definitely did not want to make my mother privy to this girl's determination to be married by the time she finished college. (She did manage to get married before she finished college, to a man she met in England at summer school in Oxford in 1958.) To break off with this friend would be more difficult for me if I had easy access to Wellesley. So I decided I did not want a car. Ilse was quite annoyed when I refused to get a car on the grounds I was too busy to bother with keeping a car. She rightly suspected this was not the whole story. She wrongly suspected I simply wanted to avoid being used to drive my mother and grandmother when I was home on vacation.

CHAPTER 51:

Her Driving

The summer of 1957 we stayed in Ellsworth, Maine in Paul and Susie's house, which was available as their family had gone to Europe. I drove the Schrag's blue Plymouth and gave my mother driving lessons. Giving someone driving lessons if they are not a naturally adept driver is tricky, but it brings one close together. What I had to do was give my mother some practice, but I also had to be her psychologist and make her understand that she needed to be calm and totally in control of her emotions when she was behind the wheel. She was fine at staying within lines, steered well, and eventually learned to pass cars with judgment if the stretch ahead was straight, long, and fully visible. She did not speed. We did not work on parking very much, as in those days in Ellsworth there was no need to parallel park. The problem that I worried about and which we practiced a great deal was entering onto a highway from a smaller road. If there was traffic and one had to wait until the traffic abated, Ilse would become impatient. She had this idea that there should be equity and fairness among drivers, and that if she had waited for a while the traffic on the main road should give her a turn. "Jetzt kann ich gehen" ("now I can go" or "now it's my turn"), she would say, assuming that the oncoming cars had good manners and knew she had been waiting to enter the highway and that there was some commitment to "taking turns." She eventually understood the concept of "right of way," and that "right of way" has no relationship to "taking turns," and that drivers with the right of way are not interested or aware that she had been sitting there for quite a while waiting for the traffic to abate. I taught her to make right turns and not to make left turns onto busy highways.

She began to drive, and did pretty well for many years. But there were mishaps. In 1968 I received a call from my mother. She and Karl had brought Kathy and Larry to Bangor Airport, and Larry said he would move to Canada if he were drafted and forced to go to Viet Nam. My mother did not keep her emotions under control that day. She drove off the road on the way back to Deer Isle; the car had turned over, and the rental car was a total loss. Karl and she were banged up but were not seriously hurt. She only called me the day after this event.

The road from their farmhouse to North Deer Isle Road was unpaved until recently. During my mother's lifetime, it was a narrow dirt road just less than a mile long with gullies on both sides much of the way. If my mother met another car on that road she veered to the side. She was not adept at backing up for any distance, so she could not or would not retreat to a turnoff or wider place on the road. By veering to the side of the road, she would drive into a ditch three or four times every summer. Her car did not have four-wheel drive, and she would ask a neighbor to call the garage down the road to come and pull her car out of the ditch. I feel some gratitude towards that garage, and every summer that I am in Deer Isle I buy gas there and say hello to "Pearl," the man who owned the garage and the tow truck and who had repeatedly rescued my mother.

There were concerns as my mother got older. Daniel came back from Deer Isle and said his grandmother was no longer safe on country roads at night; she did not stay on the right. I encouraged Karl and Ilse to drive only in daylight. They stopped driving back from seeing Paul and Susie in Ellsworth at night, but continued to drive locally in Deer Isle at night as they did not want to limit their social life. I warned my mother to turn the car as soon as she arrived when it was still daylight. When she left after dark she would then be able to go directly forward. Then one year I got a call saying that on leaving a concert at Kneisel Hall in Blue Hill, she drove to Bucksport instead of to Deer Isle as she had gotten lost in the dark. Nothing really bad ever happened, and the people of Deer Isle were always tolerant of Ilse's parking in the village, which often was not at all close to the curb. We all were lucky. I think of my mother and her driving these days whenever I drive to Boston and get to where interstate highway I-90 meets Route #128 and Route #30. My mother said on several occasions, after driving to see her daughter who lives just near the intersection of these three highways, that it was easy to get confused there. I agree; it is easy to get lost there.

After the blue Plymouth which they had bought from Paul and Susie wore out, my parents would fly to Bangor and rent a car there for the summer. Renting a car for ten or twelve weeks was a significant financial transaction for the car rental people in Bangor. They wanted the business and therefore were very accommodating. But my parents were not easy to please. I was with them on one occasion when they arrived at the airport and rented a car. The car arrived and my mother objected to the interior, explaining she was used to driving a Chrysler Motors car and the gear shift and design on the car they brought was confusing. They found a Chrysler Motors car but it was a robin's-egg blue. Ilse explained that Mr. Schrag was an artist and a car of that color would not look good parked in the meadow outside his studio. The next car was bright red and that did not seem suitable either. Finally they arrived with a light grey car that was acceptable. I was impressed that the car rental people remained polite and considerate until the right car was found. Karl and Ilse were very particular as to what was and what was not welcome on their farm in Deer Isle. Ilse was very protective of Karl, and this included protecting him from her nephew Albert and his wife Susanne, who were told that they and their large new red camper, about which they were very enthusiastic, were not welcome as the camper would ruin the view of the meadow. I do not think relations between Albert and my mother were ever quite as close after that. Years earlier, when Albert had gone to a camp in Maine, he and his friend David Alpers would always come to visit us in Friendship for a day or two, and Albert and I remembered my folks as having been very hospitable. But then he was a young man or a boy of less than twenty and I was no more than sixteen, and Karl and Ilse were younger too.

CHAPTER 52:

Three Generations:
Franz, Frank, and Frankie Kneisel

In Castine in the summer of 1948 we lived across the street from a man named Frank Kneisel. He was the son of the famous European violinist Franz Kneisel, who was born in Bucharest Rumania, studied in Vienna, worked in Berlin, was assistant conductor of the Boston Symphony Orchestra and violinist for the Boston Symphony Orchestra for about twenty years, was the first head of the violin Department of The Institute for Musical Arts (which later became the Julliard School of Music), and was founder of Kneisel Hall and School of Music in Blue Hill, Maine. He also played the flute, clarinet, and trumpet. Frank Kneisel (Franz's son), and his sister, Marianne Kneisel, a violinist, did not get along; Marianne said her brother was not a good enough violinist to play at Kneisel Hall. The sister had married a wealthy banker named Felix E. Kahn, who was a Director of Paramount Pictures, and they were prime movers in the establishment, administration, and support of Kneisel Hall in Blue Hill. She and her husband summered in Blue Hill. Frank Kneisel, the son who lived across the street from us in Castine in 1948, practiced a great deal and gave a concert in a renovated barn in Castine. Karl asked why he had to go; he had been hearing this man practice the pieces for this concert all summer. The sound of Frank Kneisel practicing on his violin carried across the street to our house, and it had disturbed Karl as he was painting. But he and Ilse went to the concert.

Mr. and Mrs. Frank Kneisel had a son, ten year old Frankie Kneisel, who was exactly my age and was also my best and closest friend that summer. He and I played badminton after supper every evening. We would play after it was dark until we were finally called in for bed. In those days Karl and Ilse often played badminton with us; it was a game they liked and were good at. Frankie and I went into business together that summer picking blueberries, and sold two quarts of freshly picked blueberries to his mother, charging fifty cents for each quart. My mother objected, said we could not charge Frankie's mother, and made us give the money back. I tried to explain to my mother that Frankie's mother wanted to buy the blueberries from us after we had told her we were going to walk down the street and offer them to whoever wanted to pay our price. But my mother said, "No matter." The money was returned.

During the thirty-five summers they spent in Deer Isle (1960-1995), Karl and Ilse often went to Sunday afternoon concerts at Kneisel Hall. After my mother's death, friends in Deer Isle contributed some money and endowed a chair in the concert hall at Kneisel Hall in her honor. A bronze plaque with her name on it is on the back of that chair. This came to my attention the last time I went to a concert at Kneisel Hall (where I only go if social considerations/friends require that I go). I sat through the concert directly behind a chair that had a plaque attached to the back of it that read "Ilse Schrag."

I seldom go to concerts as I have difficulty with keeping my mind from wandering after I listen to the first few notes, but that day it was still harder to concentrate on the music. (I note that the plaque actually got my mother's name wrong; it read "Ilsa," but I believe Kathy has since then had this corrected.)

CHAPTER 53:

"You May Be Smarter Than I Thought You Were": a Compliment to Jeanette's Chutney

Ilse liked Jeanette. I remember when my mother first tasted Jeanette's chutney. She took a bite, then took another spoonful. Then she said to me, "You may be smarter than I thought you were." Basically Ilse was happy that I was happy. She also asked me about Jeanette's mother shortly after she had met Jeanette. I was a bit concerned how Ilse would react to hearing that my mother-in-law had been married five times— widowed once by the death of her first husband, Jeanette's father, and then divorced four times as the following four marriages did not hold up. But Ilse simply said, "That happens." My mother was also respectful toward Jeanette. When my mother and I had tea or coffee together on Tuesdays and Thursdays, Ilse would say around 6:00 or 6:15 that it was time for her to let me go home to Jeanette. And in 1989, when I was hospitalized overnight for the repair of an inguinal hernia, Ilse called and asked Jeanette if it was O.K. for her to come to see me that afternoon in the hospital, explaining she got nervous whenever I was operated on or was hospitalized. My mother gave Jeanette a wooden Chinese checkers board, with pieces carved in such a way that a blind person can play as the pieces of each of the different colors have tops that are cut uniquely for that color. Ilse found this at the League for the Blind; I suggested Jeanette might like it, and we now play Chinese checkers on that board frequently.

CHAPTER 54:

Encounter with the Law

During the Reagan administration, an important federal judge who was appointed to the Supreme Court on the theory that he would uphold conservative causes had to withdraw as numerous witnesses had seen him smoking marijuana twenty or more years before. Shortly thereafter there was a crackdown on judges who aspired to higher office but who ignored some minor legal technicality. Another federal judge had to give up an appointment as she had not paid social security for her housekeeper/cleaning lady. Ilse, then about eighty years old, read the newspaper daily and called to ask me if she might get into trouble for not paying social security for her helpers. I asked her if she were running for public office, wanted to become a judge or the Attorney General, or had other political aspirations. If not, then she should not worry and leave things as they were. Asking me for legal advice was not a great idea, but I thought I could risk giving her this advice.

But once Ilse almost did land in jail. She had numerous unpaid tickets from the department of sanitation, who fined or ticketed owners of homes whose garbage pails had been spilled and if the spilled garbage had not been cleaned up. My mother knew it was a habit of kids from the nearby school to overturn garbage pails just as a prank and to make a mess, and this often resulted in her getting a fine/ticket from the sanitation inspector. She thought justice demanded that she not have to pay all these fines, and perhaps also hoped a complaint against the kids or school might be of value or a public service. The judge in the city court who listened was not the least bit interested in Ilse's very precise and careful story and told her to pay all the delinquent tickets/fines or stay in jail until they were paid. He or the court would only accept a cash payment. My mother did not have enough cash and only a phone call to Raymond's law office to come with cash prevented her from spending the night (at age eighty, no less) in jail.

CHAPTER 55:

Medical Problems

In the early 1970s I came over to my parents' house for tea one Sunday afternoon. She and Karl had been talking. My mother looked as though she had been upset, and she said to Karl, somewhat excitedly as I recall, that she did not think she had to go to the doctor for a checkup. I listened and then said getting a checkup once a year was not a bad idea and perhaps she should go for a checkup. "When did you last see Dr. Hauser?" I asked. (Dr. Daniel Hauser was my mother's internist, as well as the internist for Kathy's in-laws.) Two or three days later my mother called me to tell me she had gone to the doctor; he had found a lump in her breast, the lump was malignant, and she would need a mastectomy. I said I was sorry, but it was good they found it early. She said I seemed to have psychic powers, as evidently I must have surmised that there was a problem and I obviously knew she needed help. I asked her if she knew she had a lump in her breast and had discovered it herself. She denied she had known of the lump before she saw Dr. Hauser. But I did not believe her. I think she had found the lump and had tried to avoid dealing with it. I came in just as she and Karl were discussing whether she needed to see a doctor, and I realized she was trying to avoid consulting a doctor. Once I said she was looking a bit "frumpy" (from middle English *fromple*, i.e. "wrinkled") and should see a doctor, she consented to see Dr. Hauser. There is no other good explanation for her having been upset while talking to Karl as I arrived. My mother's mastectomy was done by my colleague Dr. Frank Gump at Columbia, and she did well. She remarked to me often over the next two decades that she was glad she had had a mastectomy, as she noticed that all her friends who had had "lumpectomies" had died from recurrent breast cancer.

My mother did not really trust doctors. When I showed her the Harvard Medical School in 1959 when she was in Boston, she said, "Do you really want to get involved with all that?" She almost always accompanied Karl when he went to see a doctor. She felt he needed another person to interpret what the doctor really had said or had meant. She once said of Karl with some exasperation, "He goes to the doctor and then comes home and does exactly what the doctor tells him to do. That makes no sense; you need to interpret what he said and apply his recommendations properly by modifying them." But when she or Karl were seriously ill, they were surprisingly cooperative and were quite good patients, but only after they had accepted the inevitability of needing professional medical attention.

Karl had had rheumatic fever as a child. The doctors could diagnose that he had aortic valve insufficiency by listening to his heart with a stethoscope. His mother was solicitous of him, as he was her "sickly child." As he was born in 1912 and grew up long before penicillin was available, recurrent sore throats were a hazard for him, and there was reason for concern. (Both Karl and Ilse were the youngest of the family, and both were catered to and spoiled because each of them had had serious medical problems.) In the early 1940s, Karl was rejected by the draft because of his heart murmur. He told me once with a smile, "They thought of putting me in a tank until they listened to my heart." In the 1960s Karl saw my senior colleague, Dr. James Leland, who told him about his heart murmur and that he would one day need to have something done about the aortic valve. Karl said he did not like Dr. Leland and saw him only once. Karl's doctor was Julian Hyman, whom Karl chose as he was an admirer and collector of Karl's work and Karl thought someone who appreciated his work would take better care of him and understand him better than someone else. (Karl felt particularly comfortable with doctors he had picked because of their interest in his work.) Julian and George Hyman were brothers; both were hematologists/oncologists, and Julian never pushed Karl to consider heart surgery. Karl had also been told by several doctors in Maine that he had a heart problem. In fairness to my mother's and Karl's reluctance to have Karl undergo open heart surgery to have his aortic valve replaced, I should mention that aortic valve replacement was not done routinely, safely, or easily until the early 1970s. By the mid-1980s aortic valve replacement was a fairly standard procedure.

By 1986 Karl was getting short of breath. At first he had to walk slowly up stairs, but eventually he could barely walk up the stairs in his home. Karl and Ilse planned a vacation to Jamaica and we had supper together in a restaurant a week or so before they were to leave. My mother said to me, "So you give your permission for us to go to Jamaica for two weeks?" I said, "No, I do not. If you go to Jamaica it's your business. I think Karl needs to be catheterized and may need heart surgery as he is readily short of breath." My folks decided not to go to Jamaica, or so my mother told me in a phone call a few days later. Two or three weeks later, Karl had to be hospitalized. He had no choice; he was suddenly unable to breathe. Dr. John Walsh was the heart surgeon at Lenox Hill Hospital who was called in to see Karl. Paul and Ilse could not accept that Karl needed surgery and suggested more consultations. I recall telling Paul, who recommended getting more consultations, that there came a time in a man's life when he could not be helped by a brother, an accountant, a lawyer, more consultants, or a wife, but needed to be taken into the operating room and have his chest opened up by an aggressive cutting heart surgeon. I can still hear my poor uncle saying to me, "You mean it is as bad as that?" Actually it was a bit trickier; Karl was in pulmonary edema (congested lungs from heart failure) and the Lenox Hill doctors were urging Dr. Walsh to take Karl to the operating room. I had been in this business for a while (I of course was not Karl's doctor), and knew Karl was in no shape to survive surgery that day. I said as much and the doctors agreed to postpone surgery, try to get Karl in better shape, and then reevaluate him for surgery. They asked me how would the family react if he died before he had surgery, and I said this man had been advised to have surgery previously and had refused. If he died in the intensive care room because his mitral valve had ruptured and he had waited too long, they would not be held responsible.

The next morning, after Karl had spent the night in the intensive care unit and had been treated to remove the fluid in his lungs, his lungs were almost clear. He went to the O.R. that morning and Dr. Walsh replaced both the mitral and the aortic valves. Karl recovered over the next two weeks. He complained of two things: when lying awake at night he could hear a slight noise (the clicking of the new valve), and the anesthesiology people had knocked out one tooth when he was intubated. I reassured him that he had had a very good result. Ilse was happy and ordered "inclinators," sliding chairs for the staircases at their house. She felt somewhat guilty for having been a party to postponing the necessary surgery for so long. They went to Dr. Walsh's office for a follow-up visit, and while Dr. Walsh was examining Karl, Ilse approached the secretary. She asked, "Is it not true that such a big heart operation is something no one ever has except in an emergency and when it is absolutely necessary?" The secretary was a kind woman and reassured my mother she was correct. My mother explained this to me the following day. My mother used the secretary's comment as exculpatory information and to assuage her guilt for her complicity with Karl in refusing surgery and ignoring the many doctors who had advised him to deal with his heart problem.

Karl lived another nine and a half years, and had little difficulty due to his heart until the last few months of his life. A year or two after the operation I asked him whether having heart surgery had been a bad experience. He said, "No, it was not that bad." He did not remember having suffered. He did not like anyone mentioning to him or reminding him that he had resisted heart surgery most strenuously and against the advice of many doctors. I never even went close to that point in my conversations with him. He was actually quite proud after the surgery for having been so valiant and for being so much stronger than he had imagined he would be. Karl also praised Ilse to me, saying she had been wonderful to him when he was ill. When I left my parents' home some two or three weeks after his heart surgery, my mother took me to the door on the ground floor as it had to be locked from the inside. Just before shutting the gate she said, "It's lucky for you that Karl did not die. I would have not left you a cent." I kissed her, said we all had gone through a tough time, and added, "But he needed the surgery and he did not die."

A month after Karl had had his heart surgery, my mother called me to say that there was a show opening that coming

Saturday afternoon, and all their artist friends would be there; Karl was not yet up to going, but she would like to go and asked if I would go with her. I tried to persuade her not to bother going, citing the recent illness and surgery. But she went. In the taxi to the gallery, I asked her whether it was really so necessary for her to go to this exhibit. She said it was necessary, and when I pressed further she said, "It is very important to show them all that Karl and I are not yet dead." I said, "O.K."

Towards the end of her life my mother would occasionally say. "I am not a minimalist. It's O.K. for others to live in neatly kept apartments where every room is tidy. But we have lived in this brownstone for fifty years and when I die I will leave you a big mess. But you can take your time to clean it up and that will be your job after I die." And that is more or less what happened. For months I would spend several hours each weekend sorting through "stuff," some of which was interesting but some of which was not interesting at all. Kathy and Larry were helpful in many ways as we wrestled with the problems of cleaning up so much accumulated art and so many personal possessions. But Kathy and Larry lived in Auburndale, Massachusetts and I lived across town, so I could go to the house much more readily and work there often for a few hours at a time. In 1998 and in most of 1999, if I saw a dumpster parked on 95th Street because someone was doing construction or renovations, I would quickly find some bulky things in my parents' now-deserted house to throw into the dumpster. If it snowed, I would clear the sidewalk with a snow shovel as we were required to do. When the house had been inhabited, strong young men would ring the bell and offer to shovel the snow and clear the walk. When the house was uninhabited no one was there to hire them and, unless I was lucky enough to find one in the street working on a neighbor's sidewalk, I would have to do the shoveling myself.

My mother had various serious medical problems towards the end of her life. Dr. Hauser found an ovarian mass that turned out to be ovarian cancer. That was removed, and my mother recovered quickly and even insisted on going up to Maine shortly after this surgery. I went with them since my mother was not yet up to driving, and I stayed two or three days until they were comfortable and installed. When I drove them from Bangor Airport to Deer Isle, I took a short cut: Route #199 to North Penobscot and then Route #175 to South Penobscot, and then Route #176 until it joined Route #15. My mother said I was going the wrong way, and she was about to be very unpleasant as she did not like my being lost or that Karl and she would be inconvenienced by a detour. She suddenly saw a small roadside fruit stand she recognized and realized I was exactly on the right road. She had insisted on going to Maine before she had had much time to recover as a favor to Karl, and had not yet really recuperated from her surgery. She was still quite irritable.

My mother would tell me of her concern whenever her friends had a serious medical problem. Her real purpose was to squeeze some information out of me, which she might then discuss with her friend or the friend's spouse. I was not so happy about this, as I was commenting on information that was fed to me by my mother which might not be accurate, and certainly the information she provided was not the complete story. Nor was it in any way professional to give medical advice to my mother who might quote me to her friends. I resisted answering questions for a while. But then my mother said she was just running things by me, she would not quote me, and if her friends took her advice or liked to talk to her about their medical problems, that was no business of mine. I then let her tell me whatever she wished. Sometimes I asked a few questions, and sometimes I said I did not have enough information and could only make a guess as to what might be going on. Her questions sometimes alleviated her concerns, as she would ask me to speculate as to whether her friend's problem was likely to be happily resolved. I do not doubt that those guesses, when optimistic about the outcome, were communicated to her friends. I heard about many illnesses. Often my mother would say she had been thanked for her advice or comments. I would then say, "I hope you did not quote me." My mother felt as entitled to my medical opinions when she consulted me, as she felt entitled to give away my favorite childhood books after I was married. One day she said to me, "I understand why they sometimes have to replace the aortic valve and I understand why they might have to replace the mitral valve, but what makes them decide they need to replace both the mitral and the aortic valve?" I replied, "Mom, if you are that involved with your friends' problems, you should send them a bill and make sure they pay it."

In 1990, when Ilse was eighty, she told me she had had an echocardiogram at the request of Dr. Hauser and had a narrow (stenotic or obstructed) aortic valve. I urged her to undergo cardiac catheterization. We discovered her coronary arteries were perfectly fine and were wide open, which was important and necessary information before replacing the aortic valve. Fixing the aortic valve and the coronary arteries should and would have been done at the same time if it had been necessary to fix the coronary arteries. Ilse also had a normal cholesterol. Friends envied the normal cholesterol level and wondered how, after all that butter, cheese and the many desserts she had eaten, her cholesterol could be normal. Ilse said, "I was born before cholesterol was invented." The week following the cardiac catheterization, she had an aortic valve replacement for her very constricted aortic valve outlet. Her friend and neighbor, Mrs. Arthur Ludwig, the wife of an internist on the staff at Mount Sinai Hospital, had advised my mother not to have heart surgery, telling her that at her age she might have a stroke and it was too dangerous. At the time I had found that less than helpful, but my mother knew enough not to listen to her. As with Karl, the hard part had been getting her to accept the need for surgery; once it was done she recovered quickly and did not pamper herself. Exactly seven days after the aortic valve had been replaced, I was coming out of my parents' house and Mrs. Ludwig saw me by chance just as she was leaving her house; she rushed up to me, and asked, "How is your Mom doing? I heard she had heart surgery a week ago." "Yes, exactly a week ago," I said. "But you don't have to ask me, you can ask her yourself; she's coming out this door in a moment to go with me for a little walk." Mrs. Ludwig looked at me as though I had gone crazy and I just gave her a big smile. My mother lived another seven years after having heart surgery and was glad she had had the surgery done.

CHAPTER 56:

Art Exhibits and Socializing with Artists in Deer Isle, Maine and in New York City

In Deer Isle, Karl painted in his barn and Ilse enjoyed the plum and apple trees and had Fuller Eaton plant a vegetable garden every summer for many years. My mother baked plum and apple pies from the fruit of the trees on their farm and these were delicious pies. Keeping the deer and the slugs away from the vegetable garden was a hobby of my mother's and a field of study all in itself. Putting sheep manure on the garden kept the deer away, as the deer dislike the smell of sheep manure. This fact is well known to local farmers. Keeping the slugs away was more difficult; covering the ground with plastic sheeting, spraying gasoline or linseed oil around the periphery of the garden or on a fence or on the black plastic sheeting on the ground, and using various insecticides did little good.

Karl had close friends in Deer Isle. On rainy days Leonard Baskin and his son Hosie ("Hosea" as in the prophet Hosea) would come by. Karl and Lennie would look at paintings in the barn while my mother played checkers or chess with Hosie in the house. Sometimes Karl would go to Baskin's barn/studio on Little Deer Isle. One year Karl did a full life-size portrait of Baskin. After my parents died I found many other portraits: of my mother, of me, and of Kathy, as well as numerous self-portraits. Some of these had been transformed into monotypes. In many of these portraits the subject was wearing a hat which delineated the face. There were several portraits that were made into prints and a few portraits that were drawings. Although I own many portraits of Karl and Ilse, I do not hang any in my home as they make me a little sad. I had been under the surveillance of my parents for so long that I decided that having their portraits hanging in my home watching over me was not necessary.

There were only three times when I remember Karl as being unhappy in Deer Isle. Once was when Sally Lund was found to be seriously ill with an incurable illness. The second was when he saw that the large pine tree, which stood alone in the middle of the large meadow at the rear of the house and which he had painted or drawn often, had toppled over because its trunk had rotted. I tried to cheer him up by saying one should not mourn a tree. My mother gave me a dirty look that said, "What do you doctors know." The third time he was unhappy was when he learned his friends Leonard and Lisa Baskin had sold their place in Little Deer Isle and would be moving to England to collaborate with the poet Ted Hughes. Unhappiness was harder for him to deal with in Deer Isle, which was a retreat and a "happy place."

Towards the end of summer my parents always gave a party. They would invite forty or fifty people to look at the paintings Karl had painted in the course of the summer. The group would assemble in the large barn and then Karl would bring out, one by one, an assortment of paintings. There were night skies, meadows in sunlight or in moonlight, large trees, bouquets of flowers, ocean scenes or shorelines with rocks and trees, an occasional interior, an occasional portrait or a figure standing in the landscape or in an interior. The most astute comments came regularly from Sally Lund, and after she died the comments were distinctly less interesting as no one related to the work as well as Sally. After all the paintings had been shown, we had food and drinks. My mother served homemade apple and blueberry pies, crabmeat salads, and lobster salads, and there was good wine, and it was a happy event. My folks tended to schedule these gatherings when I came as they expected me and Jeanette to help. I did not mind helping clear some dishes and serving wine, but neither Jeanette nor I wanted to be used to give a party for my folks. Inviting fewer people was out of the question. I recall telling my mother late in her life that she was older now, and she could no longer serve homemade pies, and the days of crab salad and lobster rolls were over; we would offer cheese and crackers, pretzels, wine, potato chips, and cookies and let it go at that. Ilse said she could not do that. I asked, "Why not?" "People will think I am senile," was her answer. I forget exactly what happened, but the end result was a compromise.

Karl had an exhibit of his work every two or three years at the Kraushaar Gallery. My parents always gave a party after the opening. My mother was always torn as they planned this party as to whether she would or would not include her side of the family, who were not among Karl's "artist friends." Her brother was offended if and when he was excluded. He always reminded my mother that he had saved her from having to spend the Second World War in Beirut. I once heard him say to my mother, "Do you have the Kurt Waldheim syndrome?"—Kurt Waldheim being the former Secretary General of the United Nations who had amnesia regarding his whereabouts in 1942 when he was serving as an officer with Nazi army units that committed war crimes. The implication was that Ilse should remember her brother with gratitude and include him. He dealt with many people with whom he did business, and he reacted with his businessman's mentality, i.e. the perception that slights were a threat to doing further business together, whenever he perceived himself to have been slighted. My parents just wanted to give a party and invite their artist friends with whom Karl wanted to celebrate, and offending Henry and Margot was never really my mother's or Karl's intention. Nonetheless, whether to include my mother's family and to what degree when there was a party to celebrate the opening of Karl's exhibition at Kraushaar Gallery was always an awkward issue and was never resolved to everyone's satisfaction. When torn between loyalty to Karl or loyalty to her brother, Ilse would always choose to follow Karl's wishes irrespective as to whether her brother was annoyed or not. At her brother's eighty-fifth birthday party, given by his son at the Century Club of New York, my mother stood up and gave a very nice talk praising Henry's acumen and wisdom, but then saying that she had been the little sister for all her life and that her brother's children and grandchildren should know that there were many things about which her brother was not well-informed and about which they knew much more than he did. My mother was aware her intelligence had been underrated by her brother but had accepted it, and was advising the younger people to have more confidence in their own intelligence and ability.

CHAPTER 57:

My Mother and I are Forced to Admit We are Still a Bit German (Whether We Like It or Not)

In 1989 East and West Germany were reunited. My mother was happy about it. I chided her saying she had been in the USA since 1938, more than half a century, and the reunification of Germany should not be of any importance to her by now. She said it was only right that Germany be reunited. I said to her, "I know why you are so happy; deep inside you are just a Prussian lady and a devoted fan and follower of Bismarck." She smiled and said, "Maybe so." I thought of this in recent years after my younger son brought to my attention that I could become a German citizen. I had no need or desire to be a German citizen. I had no need to work in Germany and did not even need to work at all any more. But Jonathan explained that, under German law, anyone deprived of their German citizenship in 1941 (all political refugees of German nationality living outside of Germany were deprived of their nationality) could claim German citizenship. The law of 1941 was rescinded in 1951 and declared to have been illegal. Not only was I entitled to claim German citizenship (as both my parents were German citizens when I was born and as my birth certificate was registered with the German Consulate of Beirut, Lebanon and stamped with a German eagle), but once I was a German citizen all my descendants could also claim German citizenship. My son said I could enable his daughters to work in the European Union if they wished and that might be a useful gift. I still had some problems and reservations with this and wondered how I would feel watching old war movies and thinking that after all that I was now a German. But I went ahead and am now a citizen of the USA as well as of Germany. To my considerable surprise, tears came spontaneously to my eyes when I was handed my German Certificate of Citizenship (*Einbuergerungsurkunde*). The tears came, I believe, not because I was happy or grateful but because it was eighty years since my mother had fled from Germany, and much had been destroyed and turned into rubble and much had also improved or been rebuilt in the interval. I wondered what Karl and Ilse would have said on hearing I had become a German (as well as remaining an American) citizen. I think they would have understood and would have had no objections. Refugees are different from other people; they live in multiple worlds, much as children who have multiple parents because of divorce or adoption. I recall an evening in my home in the early 1990s when my wife's son Benjamin brought along a friend and the friend's girlfriend. This girlfriend was a well-educated young woman who lived in Berlin and spoke a perfect contemporary Berlin German, a very precise, clearly enunciated, sophisticated modern German. Karl and Ilse were with us that evening and my mother listened to this woman intently and with pleasure as they spoke in German.

My mother worried a great deal about the illnesses of her

friends as they aged. But she managed to keep her concerns under control. One day she said to me, "I have stopped worrying. I discovered I am always worrying about the wrong thing." She remained quite realistic even in her last years. When she had painters paint the rooms in her house, she said to me with equanimity, "I only do this every ten years and I am now eighty-six; this is the last time I will need to go through this inconvenience." She had a remarkable ability to not be disconcerted when people were annoyed with her. She seldom let people upset her when they were critical of her. She ascribed someone's annoyance to the person's having a personal problem or a bad day. In this she was often correct, but not quite as often as she believed herself to be correct. I think I heard her say, "Questions are never indiscreet, only the answers are indiscreet" several hundred times. I do not believe this at all; it was just an excuse she provided for herself to excuse her probing and asking unwelcome questions.

CHAPTER 58:

Getting Older and More Dependent: "Since When Are You the Boss?"

The summer of 1996 my mother spent in New York City, as she was not well enough to go to Maine. In June of 1997 she was well enough to go to Maine, and wanted to go very much. I visited her one day and explained how this would happen. She and her caretaker, Barbara, would fly up to Bangor where Jeanette and I would meet them. She and Barbara could stay in Deer Isle for ten days. Jeanette and I would leave them after a few days and return to New York so we could pick them up when they flew back from Bangor to New York. Kathy and Larry would be there for the last several days that they were there, and would drive my mother and Barbara from Deer Isle to Bangor. My mother listened to all this and said, "Since when are you the boss?" I laughed and said that if she agreed, she could get to Deer Isle with the help I had arranged; if not, she had a nice comfortable home in Manhattan. My mother then agreed with the plans, as she wanted to go to Deer Isle. Barbara and my mother flew together to Bangor, Maine. As my mother was about to get off the plane in Bangor, the airport personnel wheeled up a wheelchair for her to use as she came down the staircase at the exit of the plane. She waved them away saying, "I have plenty of problems but walking is not one of them." Old friends and acquaintances in Deer Isle were happy to see her. Ilse said, "They are happy to see me because they thought I was dead." She enjoyed the time in Deer Isle. I saw her a few days after her return to New York and Ilse said to me, "You were right. Ten days was just enough and just right."

CHAPTER 59:

Final Illness, Death, and Privacy Issues

A brief word about my mother's final illness: it was merci-
fully short. Shortly before Thanksgiving she fell at home
and broke her hip, had surgery, and had what was essentially an intra-operative death that occurred while they were
working on her hip. Because of an episode of prolonged hypotension during the operation, she was "brain dead" when
she was placed in the postoperative recovery room. After
my mother was comatose or "brain dead" for several days,
her caretaker Barbara called to say her mother was visiting
from Guyana and was a practitioner of Voodoo. Barbara said
she had spoken to her mother who wanted to try to help my
mother, and asked if her mother could come and try to resus-
citate my mother using some Voodoo methods. Kathy and I
discussed this on the phone. We do not believe in Voodoo,
but decided Barbara's offer was well-meant and motivated
by affection and an inability to accept my mother's terminal
condition. We agreed Barbara could come with her mother to

visit our mother. "Voodoo is as good as anything the medical doctors have to offer at this point," I remarked to Kathy. "But what if it works?" Kathy and I speculated while laughing a bit nervously. "Then Ilse will really have a valid complaint against the medical profession," I answered. Barbara's mother came, but her Voodoo did not work. My mother died about a week later. I knew she had had multiple medical problems even before her hip broke, and that the boundaries of my mother's independence had been steadily contracting for some time. My daughter reviewed the hospital chart after my mother died and said, "Dad, they did their best. There was no malpractice." I had Deborah review this as I was too involved to trust my judgment. I had obsessed a bit about what had happened; I knew hypotension is a predictable complication at a certain moment when one is replacing a hip, and doubted that using epidural anesthesia for a total hip replacement was appropriate as hypotension can be much harder to control in the presence of epidural anesthesia. (The epidural anesthesia blocks the nerve mechanisms that could otherwise have been stimulated to increase the blood pressure.) I was told that using epidural anesthesia was done commonly, which did not address the appropriateness of using it for my elderly mother. I thought they showed poor judgment, and a jury might or might not think this was foolish enough to amount to "malpractice" if a good lawyer were to explain to a jury why this had been foolish. But I also knew that my grief made me think that what had happened was not acceptable. Grief colors one's judgment and I have always believed that medical malpractice lawsuits are often generated by grief and unacceptable loss rather than by valid (as opposed to perceived) wrongdoing on the part of doctors.

My kids were very considerate of me the week after my mother died. Daniel called and asked me to play tennis with him, and both Deb and Jon called me twice a day for a few days. My cousin Peter Samton called to say the obituary notice in the *New York Times* failed to mention his father, my mother's brother; would I please correct this? I did correct this for the next day's paper. But I was still angry and grieving and thought to myself, "My poor mother. Even after her death and in her obituary she has to be deferential and obedient to the wishes of her big brother." There were lots of phone calls from relatives. Jennifer called after the first week to say she had a terrible weekend without any work and missed not only my mother but "missed the abuse." We had had a small gathering at the house just after my mother died and I did fine, with my emotions well under control, until Jennifer hugged me and said she was family now, and was crying in an almost uncontrolled way which then made it impossible for me not to cry too.

I remembered to invite Mrs. Maude Eaton, who was almost exactly the same age as my mother, to my mother's memorial service so she could see Dan, Deb, and Jon. She had been our housekeeper when my children were young, had not seen them in a long time, and knew my mother well. During the years Mrs. Eaton had worked for my family, my mother often spoke to her and often gleaned information from her or tried to glean information about whatever interested my mother at the time about our household. But Mrs. Eaton would report to me what my mother had asked about and could be relied on to withhold information despite my mother's inquisitiveness. Mrs. Eaton was wily and an expert at feigning ignorance when she did not want to answer a question, and was resilient to my mother's probing. Often they spoke to arrange something for my children. My mother would occasionally give Mrs. Eaton sweaters and shawls and scarves, and now and then some extra money at holiday time. Ilse appreciated that Mrs. Eaton was devoted to my family. I had continued to see Mrs. Eaton when I lived alone on 110th

Street. She lived nearby and came to clean my apartment for half a day every week from 1980 to 1985. Mrs. Eaton had been under my care when she had a severely infected gallbladder. I had taken care of her husband George, who had poor circulation to his legs causing him to have both legs amputated. Over the years Mrs. Eaton and I became friends. I also spoke with my mother's childhood friend Hanni, who lived in London, and who used the call to talk to me about her memories of my mother's father, whom she had known well.

My mother was not dead for long before I got inquiries about her house. My cousin Peter, a successful architect, offered either to buy it, or to help sell it, or to find someone to live in it. This was not helpful. The cleaning out of the house would take another two years and I said as much to my cousin. Kathy and I were aware that someone would be interested in renovating this large old house and then could sell it for a high price. We also knew realtors wanted to earn a large commission for its sale. But I explained to my cousin and several others that we would not be rushed and would find our own agents. Some realtors were amazingly persistent, even calling Raymond Schrag, my parents' lawyer, rather than me. In one case I recall having to say to Raymond that I would not do business with that particular realtor who had harassed my mother with phone calls when my mother was alive. He had persisted in forcing himself on us, even after I had asked him to leave us alone. He simply assumed the right to sell the property belonged to him. My mother had actually handled this man quite well on her own. She had remarked to me that he kept calling her and would say he could sell her house and she would get a million dollars. "And what do you say to him?" I asked my eighty-six-year-old mother. She answered, "I tell him to send me a letter and put his proposals in writing." Then my mother smiled; both she and I knew that by then all her mail came to me and would only reach her after I had sorted it, opened it, and reviewed it.

There is little privacy in the modern world. After the brownstone in which my parents had lived for fifty years (from June 1947 to November 1997) was sold, neither Kathy nor I were particularly eager to share with everyone the selling price of our parents' former home. Karl and Ilse most certainly would not have wanted to publicize the price for which their house was sold. When friends and family asked how much money it had been sold for, we would say that we got a reasonably good price for it according to the realtor. Then some months after it had been sold, there was an article in the Sunday *Times* real estate section, showing a picture of the front of the house and giving the address. The article said this brownstone had recently been sold for 1.85 million dollars. So much for keeping secret the selling price of my parents' home.

I wrote a letter to Dr. Daniel Hauser, her internist, after my mother died. I thanked him for his help over the years. I had met him but only once—and then very briefly—but I respected his judgment. My mother was not an easy person to care for. She did not like seeing her dentist, dermatologist, radiologist, surgeons, the doctors who treated her depression and her episode of paranoia (which required ECT, "electro-convulsive therapy," which was highly effective and restored her to "normal" within two days, and which is the treatment of choice for severe depression in the elderly), nor Dr. Hauser in follow-up. If my mother was kept waiting in their offices she became "restless." Also there were a few too many visits by her social worker, who seemed reluctant to accept that Barbara and Jennifer were managing well and did not need her supervision. Kathy and I persuaded Raymond to give Barbara, Jennifer, and Naomi, the social worker, generous "termination" checks. All three were very happy with what they received. I was left thinking old people are vulnerable to being abused or cheated or taken advantage of, but no one cheated or took advantage of my mother to any significant degree.

A few weeks after Ilse had died, I was in my office and listened to some old messages that had been stored on my answering machine. It was an eerie experience to hear my mother's voice and several messages from her that described some pressing problem. I decided not to erase those messages immediately thinking that perhaps I might like to be able to listen to my mother's voice. But after the second time I listened to them I erased all the messages. I also have a CD-Video taken at my uncle Paul's eightieth birthday party in 1989, which records all the people in attendance as they take their places around the table at the birthday party. I played it once but will not play it or look at it again. I prefer to deal with people and events in real time and not to see them so vividly after they are dead.

After my parents died and their house was sold, I never again needed to be on 95th Street between Lexington Avenue and Park Avenue. It is a residential area that I am no longer connected with, and I have avoided that block which I had frequented for over fifty years. I also avoided the "Y" at 92nd Street and Lexington Avenue. My mother had gone there often over many years. I tended to avoid the places she frequented. But there are other places that make me think of my mother. Occasionally I need to be near Hunter College, and I notice the awning which indicates the entrance to the Karl and Bertha Leubsdorf Library. I am one of the few people in New York City who knew and remembers Karl and Bertha Leubsdorf. They were the parents of Carl Leubsdorf (my classmate some sixty-five years ago in grades five through eight at P.S.6) and Johnnie Leubsdorf, Carl's little brother. Carl was the smartest kid in my class and a playmate in Central Park, where a group of us played football after school. Carl is now a political reporter for a newspaper in Texas. His brother John is a law professor at Rutgers. My mother and their mother, Bertha Leubsdorf, first met when I was in public school and they stayed in touch long after Carl and I lost contact, as both women often went to the "Y" at 92nd Street. Ilse was still going to the "Y" for French lessons during the last two years of her life and after Karl died. She explained to me that she liked taking French classes as she already knew French, and she liked the teacher, a ninety-year-old woman, who was blind but spoke excellent French, and who was, as my mother put it, "worse off than I am." A few years before she died, my mother wondered what to do with the fifty-volume edition of the complete works of Honoré de Balzac in French, which had been a present from Karl; he had bought this edition from his friend Lucien, a dealer in fine and rare French books. I remember those little books bound in blue leather bindings on the bookshelf in my parents' living room. Ilse called the Karl and Bertha Leubsdorf Library at Hunter and asked them if they wanted her volumes of Balzac in French. They did, and that is where those volumes are now.

CHAPTER 60:

"I Did Everything Wrong and It All Turned Out All Right"

Sometime in the last six months of her life my mother stroked my cheek and said, "I did everything wrong, and it all turned out all right." I laughed and said, "That is an oversimplification of a long and complicated story. But don't worry. We did do very well. Many German Jews fared far less well than we did in the 1930s and early 1940s." Neither Berlin nor Beirut were easy places in which to live when my mother was there. She was right to flee Berlin in 1933, and also was right to leave Beirut in 1938 to come to New York. She found Karl and had a wonderful life with him. She did all right. I told her she was not responsible for the many decisions I had made in my adult life; I had often ignored her advice or suggestions. She doubted the correctness or the appropriateness of many of my decisions, including to go to Harvard, to marry young, to become a medical doctor, to have children at a young age, to marry the daughter of a conservative rabbi, to work for a Catholic professor of medicine at Columbia University, and to go to Sydney to meet Dr. Hans Price. All these decisions of mine were inevitably complicated by subsequent problems and unforeseen consequences, but all were enthusiastically entered into at the time they were made. I have no genuine regrets, although I will admit I often could have been wiser in the way I handled subsequent problems and that I could at times have conducted myself with more finesse.

My mother made a mistake in keeping her first husband, my biological father, out of my life. But eventually I was able to meet him. When we finally did meet, my curiosity overcame whatever anger and resentment I might have had and which I had previously thought might be difficult for me to control. He and I had made deliberate choices and neither of us was apologetic for what those had been. Yet he and I were interested in each other. Each of us knew that if the times had not been so tumultuous we might have known one another better and liked each other more. Each of us was glad we eventually had a chance to meet, although no great affection developed in the short time we spent together. I thought he had had a difficult life and had survived professionally under difficult circumstances for which he deserved credit, but he also contributed to his own life being difficult in that he was arrogant, autocratic, and inflexible in many ways, and he was definitely overly secure about his own judgment. I never was close to my biological father, but my mother and I were close. We had great affection for one another and knew each other very well. Perhaps for some years we knew one another even better than anyone else who knew us, and we were devoted and helpful to one another for all the fifty-nine years we knew each other. We also were similar in many ways and loved each other.

Acknowledgments

First and foremost, thanks goes to my wife Jeanette M. Schrag. She is an excellent editor and suggested many changes and revisions. Even though I am very resistant to taking criticism or suggestions or to accepting revisions, Jeanette managed to edit much of what I wrote. I thank her for her significant, extremely helpful, and necessary contribution. We have by now spent almost half our lifetimes together, and I love her dearly and she knows it, but that this is so should also appear here in print.

My Australian half-brothers, Michael and Eddie Price, hired a writer to rework notes left by our mutual father into a book. Perhaps indirectly that book, which is autobiographical, motivated me to write about my mother to elaborate on her point of view about doctors, to comment on her first marriage and her time in Beirut, and to describe aspects of her later life.

I owe a great deal to Dr. Francis Baudry, my psychoanalyst. I first saw him in 1970. He read an early copy of this book. He encouraged me to put it into the format of a book, and I thank him for his support and encouragement.

My friend and former colleague, Dr. David Gluck, has been a loyal friend. Over many years he has not only listened to my stories but also has encouraged me to write them down. I appreciate the encouragement he gave me.

I want to thank the many patients who came to see me in the 1970s when I had an office in Washington Heights at what was then called the Columbia Presbyterian Medical Center. There was a large community of Jewish refugees who lived in the area and many were my patients. Each of them had a different story, and each story was impressive in its own way. They made me give some thought to what had happened to me and to my mother. They also made me ask myself if I was giving them enough help and support.

All photographs appearing in this book are from my personal collection of photo albums. All reproductions of drawings or paintings are of works done by Karl Schrag and come from my personal collection.

Lastly, I want to thank my step-daughter-in-law to be, Ms. Kamy Wicoff, for her help and her enthusiasm for putting my memoir into print. She referred me to her friend and editor, Brooke Warner, whose professional services brought this project to completion. Many thanks to both of you.

About the Author

Peter Edward Schrag, M.D. grew up in Manhattan. He attended P.S. 6, which was then on Madison Avenue and 85th Street, from grades five through eight and graduated from there in 1951. He went to high school at Friends Seminary and graduated in 1955. He has an A.B. (cum laude in mathematics) from Harvard College (1959) and an M.D. from Harvard Medical School (1964). With the exception of the two years he worked as an officer in the U.S. Public Health Service and was stationed in Raleigh, North Carolina (1966-1968), he has always worked as an internist in Manhattan. He has three children by his first marriage: Deborah Schrag, Daniel P. Schrag, and Jonathan E. Schrag, who live in Cambridge and Boston, Massachusetts with their families. Dr. Schrag and his wife Jeanette live at 250 West 94th Street in Manhattan. (Note: Peter Edward Schrag, M.D. is not to be confused with—but conceivably could easily be confused with—Peter Schrag, his cousin, who is an author and journalist and lives in Oakland, California.)

77624614R00163